One life, two stories

Nancy de Vries' journey home

Nancy de Vries
Gaynor Macdonald
Jane Mears
Anna Nettheim

DARLINGTON PRESS

Published 2012 by Darlington Press
Darlington Press is an imprint of Sydney University Press
sydney.edu.au/sup

© Nancy de Vries, Gaynor Macdonald, Jane Mears and Anna Nettheim 2012
© Darlington Press 2012

Reproduction and Communication for other purposes

Except as permitted under the Act, no part of this edition may be reproduced, stored in a retrieval system, or communicated in any form or by any means without prior written permission. All requests for reproduction or communication should be made to Darlington Press at the address below:
Darlington Press
Fisher Library F03
University of Sydney NSW 2006 AUSTRALIA
Email: sup.info@sydney.edu.au

ISBN 978-1-921364-25-9

Cover images
Front: Nancy de Vries addresses the NSW Parliament, representing the stolen generation after NSW Premier Bob Carr led the parliament in apologising to the Aboriginal people for the treatment of them throughout Australia's history, 18 June 1997. Photo by Nick Moir, *Sydney Morning Herald*.

Back: The high wall of Parramatta Girls Home could be scaled to provide access to the creek and park beyond. Photo by Gaynor Macdonald (2000).

Cover design by Evan Shapiro, University Publishing Service.

We dedicate this publication to the children and grandchildren of Nancy de Vries and to the thousands of other Indigenous Australians who continue to suffer the intergenerational trauma stemming from the removal of children from their families.

They are all in need of witnesses.

Contents

Acknowledgements — vii
Foreword — ix

The Apology — 1
The historical context for the Apology — 13
'Too loud not to hear': responding to stories of removal — 33
My story begins ... can you possibly comprehend? — 45
Another story ... the written record — 79
Reflections on living with difference — 115
Life was pretty scary — 125
They said I wouldn't be good enough — 133
Finding Ruby — 153
The pain persists — 175
References — 193

Acknowledgements

Our thanks to the many people who have supported our work and this publication:

To Sydney University Press for responsive and supportive advice and publication
To the University of Western Sydney for providing a commemorative edition that Nancy could enjoy.

For editing, proofreading, friendship and inspiration, we thank
Katie Mears, Pat Bazeley of the Research Farm, Lisa Studach, Rebecca Macken, Daniela Heil, Margot Nettheim, Fiona Nicholl and Charlie Eldridge.

For their stories, Lynette Sheather and Judith Townsend; for their own writing, Val Wenberg and Siena Perry.

For tangible support at critical moments,
Prof. Peter Read (The University of Sydney)

To the Australian Institute of Aboriginal and Torres Strait Islander Studies for a research grant.

For permission to use photos, as credited in the text:
Mervyn Bishop's photos taken for the Liverpool Regional Museum's Aunty Nance Exhibition, 2001; the *Sydney Morning Herald*; Fiona Nicholl and David Marshall, University of Western Sydney – photos taken at the launch in 2005.

Extracts have been edited from the following publications and we are grateful to the authors for permission to use them in this way:
Read, Peter and Coral Edwards (eds). 1989. *The lost children*. Sydney: Doubleday.
Townsend, Judith and Nancy de Vries. 1995. Aborigines, nursing, and education. In G. Gray and R. Pratt (eds). *Issues in Australian Nursing* 4. Melbourne: Churchill Livingstone.

Foreword

The University of Western Sydney is where the first author and subject of this book, Nancy de Vries, undertook her tertiary education. While at the University she met her co-authors, Jane Mears (Social Policy) and Gaynor Macdonald (Aboriginal Studies/Social Policy). Later they were joined by Anna Nettheim, who had previously worked documenting stories of removal for the 1997 Inquiry into the Removal of Aboriginal Children. This collaboration makes this book more than a biography. It is one woman's journey but it is also an invitation to travel with her. The story is unique but it documents an institutionalised history of trauma and oppression which touches us all. Nancy's co-authors have had to learn what it means to bear witness to such trauma.

I am touched by the impact the University of Western Sydney had on Nancy. Admission to UWS enabled her to follow her heart and study nursing. Her excellent academic record and subsequent accomplishments make the negative assessments of her ability as a child, so clearly documented in this book, all the more shameful. Years of being told she was not good enough left her doubting herself. At university she was able to develop the intellectual, social and professional skills to begin to put this behind her. Nancy's story, told here with great courage, reminds us that we should not accept the limits others place on our potential.

Nancy became one of our most distinguished graduates in 1988. She continued to participate in our university life, including her challenging guest lectures, here as well as at the University of Sydney, which touched the lives of hundreds of students. Once you have read this book, you will no longer think of Nancy or the many others who are part of the stolen generation in the same way.

I am delighted to have the opportunity to respond to Nancy's own generosity of spirit, and I congratulate the authors for bringing this confronting but highly readable book to a wider audience.

Professor Janice Reid
Vice Chancellor of the University of Western Sydney

The Apology

Do you know what was the biggest healing moment of my life?

When Bob Carr and all those politicians apologised and let me feel they were sorry that it happened to me and they would make sure it doesn't happen again.

They apologised to all the stolen generation. You've got no idea how wonderful that was. I couldn't explain the feeling that happened that day. It was an amazing day. I felt very humble that I had been asked to step up there, where a lot of those laws had been made, and blast it at them – in a polite way, of course. But to stand there – where all those older politicians had made those laws – and say, 'This is the result of those laws that you made, this is the hurt you gave us.'

The Premier of New South Wales, Bob Carr decided he wanted to give a formal apology to the Aboriginal people and so one of the stolen generations had to be nominated and they got my name.

Everybody was saying to me that day, 'Are you nervous? Are you nervous?'

And I said, 'No – I'm not letting this lot overpower me!'

So I got a cup of tea and somebody came along and took my photo – and I dropped my cup. Had my two arms up in the air like an old brolga bird!

Well, they laughed. And Lola McNaughton – Lola Edwards she was to me – she was laughing and laughing and I'm telling her to 'Shut up.'

So all the Aboriginal people go around and up to the top floor to get into the House where the visitors sit. They took me in and I'm sitting behind the speaker – he was going to introduce me. And while I'm sitting there waiting to be introduced, I couldn't see all the members properly, but I was thinking to myself, looking up – I'd never been in there before – and I was thinking, this is where our laws were made, and the negative stuff that was done by the parliamentarians of the day that really made our people's lives hard, this is where a lot of it came from …

And then I had to get up.

I asked the speaker what to do. He was such a doll and I could see he was getting a bit of a roast from the Opposition. But he was very honest and open when I was talking to him – that's how I found him anyway – he wasn't putting me down because I was going to be talking, he was speaking to me as an equal.

'Now when you come over here, Nancy, we do this and do that. You know you're the first woman – other than the Members of Parliament – that's spoken here in Parliament.'

I thought, 'How about that!'

He laughed then and said, 'Other than the Queen! Other than her, you're the first woman in 150 years.'

I thought, 'Wow – this is something pretty special.'

He showed me where to stand and I said, 'Righto, just quickly tell me who I've got to mention first.'

He explained, 'Well you thank me, of course, first off – Thank you, Mr Speaker – and then you say Bob Carr and then you rattle them all off, the members of the government and then you go over to the Opposition and go through them.'

Peter Collins was the boss of the Opposition then, and he's like a little boy –he's such a sweetie, he really is. And of course I knew Andrew Refshauge, and I knew the guy from Wollongong who was Secretary to the Minister for Aboriginal Affairs. And I knew our little fellow from Liverpool, Paul Lynch. So I felt quite at ease about it 'cos I knew a few of them.

So anyway, I just got up and said all that introduction, and then I had to say, 'I would like to welcome members of the Aboriginal community', because I was speaking on behalf of them. I started. 'I would also like to welcome the members of the …' – Oh, it was hard to get the words out then – and here's all these bloody blacks sitting up there, leaning forward while I'm stumbling over the words, egging me on – You could almost hear them saying 'Well, say it!' But it was so wonderful to see that whole gallery full of Aboriginal faces that it really affected me. But I got it out '… the Aboriginal Community.' That's why I had the white hanky in my hand, because it was really emotional to see them there. It was just wonderful.

The Apology

Nancy de Vries speaking to the NSW Parliament House in July 1997 before Premier Bob Carr responded with the government's Apology on behalf of generations of Aboriginal children stolen from their families. *Sydney Morning Herald* photo by Nick Moir.

So as I'm talking, I'm just telling the truth, about what a waste of bloody time it all was, and I'm asking, Why? Why did they do it? Because when I eventually got home, found my family, I was the same as them. I had a sister and a cousin who were registered nurses. My sisters, my cousins – they've all been down here to Uni, too, and they're all my family. And I said, just why? Why? What a waste.

The hurt was hanging out. I could see the men going sniff-sniff – and I thought, 'I've got them, they can hear what I'm saying.'

Bob Carr – Bob Carr's an amazing man, very reserved. He's a shy man and it tends to make him appear very cool and not really interested. But I looked at him and I thought, 'That man knows.' He knew, 'cos he's a historian too, he knew the history. And when he got up and spoke I thought, 'Thank God you're the one that's accepting this.'

And then he gave the Apology. So that was right then.

Nancy de Vries
New South Wales Legislative Assembly
18 June 1997, Parliament House, Sydney

Thank you, Mr Speaker. Premier, Leader of the Opposition, honourable members and members of the Aboriginal community. I thank you very much for the honour today to speak here in this House. I might add that this is very emotional for me; it is wonderful.

I was taken away from my mother at the age of 14 months and my journey as a lonely, homeless, unloved child began. Nobody could really understand the loneliness of an Aboriginal child in a non-Aboriginal environment who has nobody whatsoever around them, who is not treated the same as the other children in the home who are not Aboriginal, who is isolated, who is lonely, who cries at night, and who cries during the day. You could not possibly comprehend the life of that child.

Like hundreds and thousands of other Aboriginal children, I was taken away so that I could be given a better life. Believe you me, to put somebody in 22 different places before they are 18 is not giving them a better life.

When I finally reached home I found members of my family who were following the same profession. I was a registered nurse. There were members of my family who were registered nurses. There were members of my family who had been to university and who had become workers in the humanities. So, even though I was outside that family, I still had the same feelings and the same goals as my family. I can see no reason why I was ever taken away.

Growing up I had to live with people always telling me that Aboriginal people were no good, that Aboriginal people were drunks. I had no contact with Aboriginal people. I would see Aboriginal people, and I would want to run up to them and say, 'Do you know Ruby?', who was my mother, but I was not allowed to. By the time I was eight or nine I became a real rebel. I was acting out my behaviours because I was angry and I did not know what was going on in my life. I used to run away.

I took myself to Queens Square to the Department where the births, deaths and marriages registers were and asked an old man behind the counter, 'Can you please help me find my mother?' This continued on all through my life. The authorities thought it was a behavioural problem. It was not. I was searching for my identity and for my family. I needed my family.

I read my papers later in life and read what had been written about one of my foster parents. It said, 'We feel that this woman has regretted having a member of such a despised race in her family.'

The first wonderful thing that happened to me in my life was when my first child was born, my son. Suddenly I had somebody who would love me unconditionally and accept me for what I was.

When I finally got home to meet my mother after 53 years, she could not relate to me. For 53 years she had been blotting out the fact that she had lost her child. I am very much like her to look at. She was a great lady. I thank God that I got home in time to meet her and to actually speak to her. I am still not properly home yet. Because of my mother's inability to accept me again into the family, my family is very divided. But I met her.

This not only affected my life; it affected my children's lives too. They did not have a grandmother and they often used to ask me why. My son, who is 26 now and a very male person, believe you me – sometimes overly male, I think – was standing in a pub up in Bourke. One of my cousins said to David, 'Here, look, this is your uncle.' My 26 year old cried.

Thank God it is not affecting my grandchildren. Two of my grandchildren have two grandmothers who were removed but they are growing up with love, surrounded by a loving family. They are proud of their Aboriginality. They know who they are, and they know where we are going. I will protect their rights to the last breath in my body. I will never allow anything to happen to them.

I want to thank you for this opportunity to come here and share some of these experiences with you. It is very emotional for me.

I do thank you.

The Apology

Mr Bob Carr

(Maroubra – Premier, Minister for the Arts, and Minister for Ethnic Affairs)

New South Wales Legislative Assembly

18 June 1997

Parliament House, Sydney

I move:That this House, on behalf of the people of New South Wales –

(1) apologises unreservedly to the Aboriginal people of Australia for the systematic separation of generations of Aboriginal children from their parents, families and communities;
(2) acknowledges and regrets Parliament's role in enacting laws and endorsing policies of successive governments whereby profound grief and loss have been inflicted upon Aboriginal Australians;
(3) calls upon all Australian Governments to respond with compassion, understanding and justice to the report of the Human Rights and Equal Opportunity Commission entitled *Bringing Them Home*; and
(4) reaffirms its commitment to the goals and processes of reconciliation in New South Wales and throughout Australia.

The unanimous resolution of the House of 14 November last year was a landmark in this country's move to reconciliation. In moving that resolution, I referred to the national inquiry.

I extend on behalf of the Government and the people of New South Wales our apology to the Aboriginal people. We became the first Parliament to do that.

The Human Rights and Equal Opportunity Commission has now published its report. It is called "Bringing Them Home". It is a profoundly moving, deeply disturbing document. It has stirred the conscience of our nation.

> The lost generations of the stolen children have been given a voice at long last. We have been privileged to hear their message from Nancy de Vries. No more memorable or moving words have been spoken in this Parliament in the past 150 years ... We are not dealing with some abstraction from the remote past. We are confronted with continuing, contemporary pain, grief and loss, as has been demonstrated in this House this morning ...
>
> In truth, the most remarkable characteristic of the Aboriginal community, the brightest hope for the future, is absence of hatred, the faith that, despite everything, justice will prevail. That these people, who suffered such an injustice, can today deal with us without a sense of hatred is a great statement about the nature of our Aboriginal citizens, about Aboriginal people ...
>
> In conclusion, though we must always recognise the pain, always share the pain, and are always sorry for it, we must remember the progress that has been made; and this should motivate us to achieve more. Also, though we respect the solemnity of this occasion and acknowledge the importance of our apology, we must never let mere words, even important words like "sorry", overshadow our deeds. Future generations will not measure our success by just listening to our words or reading the record of this Parliament. They will look to see whether we addressed this disadvantage, whether we improved Aboriginal health and whether, in the words of the Governor-General, Sir William Deane, "Aborigine and non-Aborigine went forth together throughout the country as friends and equals, and overcame the injustice and disadvantage" which has flowed from the actions of our ancestors. If future generations realise that we did act and that we were successful, they will remember our words and deeds and regard them as perhaps this generation's greatest gift to the nation. I commend the motion.
>
> NSW LA Hansard, Art.5 of 18/6/97

The Human Rights and Equal Opportunity Commission tabled its Report, *Bringing Them Home*, in 1997. At the time, John Howard was the Australian Prime Minister, Peter Costello was Treasurer, Peter Reith was the Minister for Workplace Relations, and Senator John Herron was the Minister for Aboriginal Affairs. Kim Beazley was Leader of the Opposition.

But then, this arsehole from the National Party gets up to knock it back! All the blacks got up and walked out. They all got up and walked out. Colin Markham, he actually apologised for what was said by the Nationals. But the rest of the Opposition, they all had something positive to say. And Peter Collins, the Leader of the Opposition, he came round to me afterwards when I was sitting down the back – even when I was sitting down I was almost looking him in the eye, he's a little fellow – he came around and then he got down beside me, and he held my hand and was talking about it and he was thanking me, and he was so genuine and gentle.

And then Andrew Refshauge came over and he said to me, 'Are you all right, Nance?' Because I was starting to shake at the end of it, I was so emotional. That's why I had to sit down, because I just felt it was just too much. I thanked them and went and sat down, and that's when Andrew jumped up and came and helped me.

It was a week later I collapsed, had my heart attack. I always laughingly say to Andrew, 'It was your bloody fault, you know!'

It must never happen again …

We were taken from our families, torn from our families. The stolen generation didn't just happen in NSW. It happened all over Australia. Western Australia, Northern Territory, they were taken miles away.

I was removed from my mother when I was 13 or 14 months old – I don't know exactly. She was trying to find work, so she could take me with her. In those days it was very difficult. There was no money, she was a single parent, there was no pension, and there was the stigma of having a child 'out of wedlock', as they said politely. They stamped 'illegitimate' on your papers.

They kept on moving me and moving me and moving me. I was moved to 22 different places before I was 18. I had 22 moves, you know. Of course, a few of them were my own fault because I really was an awful child! I was a rebel. As I grew older, I got sick of people telling me that I wasn't wanted.

Having people push you away, you feel rejected and unloved. It was unbelievable the number of times I was shifted. No one looked at my records and asked why this child was moved so often.

I just wanted my mother.

They'd say to me, 'Your mother doesn't want you.' They'd say, 'Why did you run away so often?' I'd say, 'I was looking for my Mum.' 'She doesn't want you.'

I never believed it.

It makes me so angry now, people of my own generation who pooh-pooh the whole idea that the 'stolen generations' ever happened. According to them we were happy, well looked after. I get really angry because they claim they didn't even know we existed. But the thing is, they did know.

Miriam and June lived down the road from me when I was about 8 or 9. June was in my class. Miriam told me later that their mother had explained to them all those years before. She contacted me after I spoke at Parliament House. She contacted Peter Read and asked for my address. He rang and asked me first and then she wrote. June and Miriam had wanted to know why I used to cry a lot and their mother told them. That really touched me. They didn't tell me at the time. She probably told them, 'Oh, don't say anything' – you know what Mums would say – in case it hurt my foster mother. She sat her kids down and told them it was because they take Aboriginal children away from their families, and so they should be kind. That was during the war.

Their mother was always so nice to me, always kind and never stopped me playing with her kids. I said to Miriam, what a pity I didn't know all this before she died – she'd only died two years before. I could have gone and talked to her, thanked her. It meant so much to me that somebody knew and she had told her children. I don't know how she knew. Whether she'd worked it out or whether she knew of another family that had an Aboriginal child. But if this lady who lived in suburbia knew about it, did everybody else know and just shut up? Here was one lady strong enough to tell her kids what was really happening to Aboriginal children.

I go down the road and people I don't think I know say, 'Hi, how are you?' I try to go out of my way to be nice to people, to greet them and wave to them. I think that's the way we break down barriers. But to hear they were being broken down long before that by people like June and Miriam's mother – I didn't realise that.

I was watching the debate on TV and I saw Kim Beazley's emotional reaction when he was talking about reading the Report. I've got the Report. It's very heavy reading. God almighty it is! It's such a heavy book. I rang up the Telegraph and had a go about one politician calling it 'the flawed report'. No! Every one of those stories have been verified. They can be proved. I have papers to prove mine, my story.

That poor woman who just went through in NSW and got knocked back for her compensation, she's got evidence she was taken: 'The reason for removal of the child – because she is Aboriginal and fair.' But she was knocked back. She thought that through the court case she could get rid of her anger, her fear and her turmoil through her life. But it's only added to it. It was frustrating for her because she had the proof to show that what was done was quite wrong.

And Herron – the Minister for Aboriginal Affairs – said it was all legal.

My Peter laughed. He said, 'Of course it was legal. Those same bloody fools made the laws.'

You see. It was legal because they made it legal by writing these laws. It was legal to go and just take children. Oh jeez. Some of that report …

When Kim Beazley read it he wept. He wept. Oh, my heart. He was a man of power. A man in the position of power showing he cared what happened to us. He cared about it. You can't know what that means. He cried and I was overwhelmed by that.

This is what I think about Sorry Day: it's letting us know that there are people who care. Because that's half the way to healing. A few weeks later, up pops little 'Mr Sheen' – Johnny Howard – and gives a 'sincere' apology. And we've got that horrible man behind him, laughing so loudly and bending over and slapping his leg, the baldy one I mean, Peter Reith. And the other Peter sitting there, Costello, nearly dropping off to sleep. And I thought to myself, 'Sincere? How can this be a sincere apology when the rest of the government members are going on like this?' I was insulted by it. Absolutely insulted by it. It was horrible, horrible. I was screaming in my bedroom, I was going crook, you know. I just could not believe that he had the hide to say that what he said was an apology.

Herron seemed to be quite sure in his mind that we were better off. There was nothing wrong with what they did, there was nothing wrong with all my poor little mother's suffering and tears and feelings of guilt. Nothing wrong with her being unable to relate to her child when she came home – 53 years later. That was all for the best. That was all for us. They believe it.

We're all a myth … !

I suppose you've heard little Johnny and Senator Herron say that we're all a myth. Let me tell you, it definitely happened. I have all my own papers and there is not one bit of evidence that my mother signed any paper or that it went to court. I was just conveniently removed because I was Aboriginal and because my mum was Aboriginal, perhaps because I was fairer, perhaps because my mother was young, perhaps – who knows really. That's how it was then.

I just want you to know that this not only happened to me but it happened to thousands of other people. I know where sometimes five children were taken away at once. Five at once! What would that do to a mother? When you think about it, it's heart-rending. And some of these people have grown up and gone back to their families. There's one person who went back and there's a film, an actual film of her meeting her Mum. Her Mum's just sitting there and she's like a little lost soul, as if she'd shrunk. It makes you want to cry when you see it.

My hurt is very real. No amount of money could ever pay for what happened to me and what happened to my mother. And I'll tell you what, a lot of our people feel the same way, exactly the same way. There are some who feel that it is a way to get rid of our hurt and anger by claiming compensation. That is their right. If anybody gets hurt, through a car accident, through a crime, they have the right to claim compensation. But I won't.

Nancy with Carol Kendall, at a rally in Faulconbridge, 2000. The demonstration was targeting Prime Minister John Howard who was visiting the locality. It was shortly after he had refused to say 'sorry' to the stolen generations. Photographer unknown.

The historical context for the Apology

Colonisation is not an event in Australia's past. It is a process. It began at the end of the eighteenth century and Australians, Indigenous and non-Indigenous, continue to live with its impacts. We have set out a brief history here which will help to contextualise Nancy's story. We draw on some of the comprehensive studies now available so look through our references should you want to follow up on the details. Policies differed from one Australian state to another so we focus on New South Wales (for further information about laws and policies under which removal was enacted, see McRae, Nettheim, Beacroft and McNamara 2003).

The removal of Aboriginal children was a practice that started early in the story of Aboriginal people as colonial subjects. It was, and remained in its various expressions, an attempt to remove children from the influence of their Aboriginal parents who seemed, to their colonisers, to be stubbornly resistant to the benefits offered by European 'civilisation'. Only by separating the children was it thought possible to break the hold that the Aboriginal world of cultural practice and belief had on members of Aboriginal communities.

The first official school set up to inculcate Aboriginal children into white ways was the Native Institution at Parramatta, established by Governor Macquarie in 1814. It closed in 1820. Once Aboriginal parents recognised that the school aimed to distance children from their families and communities rather than educate them into new possibilities, they withdrew their children and their support (HREOC 1997:27–8, 39).

But the idea persisted that it was only in severing these bonds that Aboriginal people could be made into pliable British subjects. In time it was linked more closely to the growing interest in race theory which permeated the thought and politics of 19th-century European imperialists and 20th-century social engineers.

Despite initial setbacks, government agents and Christian missionaries removed Aboriginal children from their families and communities so as to teach them European values and work habits. Missionaries, such as those at Wellington Valley in central New South Wales in the 1830s, taught pre-initiated Aboriginal boys that their elders were 'wicked old fellows'. They believed that by separating children from their families, they could rescue them from the uncivilised ways of their parents and educate them for a

Nancy looks over the town of Cootamundra in 2004, reliving her time at the Cootamundra Girls Home run by the Aborigines Welfare Board. Photographer unknown.

better life – as servants and labourers. One of these missionaries, William Watson, became aggressive in implementing his aim. In 1838 he set up his own unofficial mission where he held and instructed children he had managed to remove from their families (Read 1999:18–20). There are many reports of Aboriginal children having been kidnapped and exploited as a source of labour throughout the nineteenth century (HREOC 1997:27).

Early relations between Aborigines and European settlers were fraught with conflict over available land and resources. Aboriginal resistance

The historical context for the Apology

to being forced off their traditional land and cut off from sources of food and water often resulted in 'punitive expeditions' in which large numbers of Aboriginal people were killed. Increasingly, as land use intensified, Aboriginal people were unable to maintain their economic and social autonomy and many were left to subsist on the fringes of the growing white communities. In the 1870s, missionaries began to lobby the government to set aside land for Aboriginal people. They also set up the missions of Maloga and Warangesda in southern New South Wales (HREOC 1997:28, 39–40). Aboriginal people too began to make their own demands for land, with stability of tenure.

Of the various scientific and philosophical theories on the nature of humanity which influenced perceptions of and treatment of Aboriginal people, 'social Darwinism' was the most influential. Positioning Aboriginal people as a less evolved 'race', which had only continued to exist through their geographical isolation, 'social Darwinism' argued that they were doomed to die out as a result of their contact with a 'superior race'.

While this 'race' theory legitimised much violence, there were also colonists who felt it was the humanitarian responsibility of the superior Christian to 'smooth the dying pillow' (Reynolds 1989:115). They called for a halt to the exploitation and maltreatment of Aboriginal people. In many areas violence did decrease, although massacres are recorded into the 1930s. There was a major setback in the recognition of Aboriginal rights after Federation in 1901. Instead of this leading to increased recognition it prompted increased segregation. In the name of protection Aboriginal people were, from then on, increasingly denied full participation in white Australia (Wolfe 1994:100) and confined on government reserves in remote and rural regions.

In 1881, a Protector of Aborigines was appointed for the colony of New South Wales and his first recommendation was for the establishment of reserve areas throughout the state. These were gazetted over the next few decades as being specifically, and solely, for Aboriginal use. In 1883, the Aborigines Protection Board was established, with one of its responsibilities being to manage these reserves as well as the Aboriginal population of New South Wales, then estimated at 9000 people.

The protectorate system in this state was based on the idea that Aboriginal people would set up self-sufficient agricultural communities on the reserve land. One rationale was that Aboriginal people would then stop hindering the processes of colonial land acquisition (HREOC 1997:28, 39–40). The reserves would also prevent them becoming a 'mendicant problem' (in other words, becoming beggars).

The aim of achieving self-sufficient Aboriginal farming communities was more successful than the Aborigines Protection Board expected. But much of this Aboriginal land was revoked under pressure from white Australians who either wanted the land once it had been made productive, or wanted the Aborigines moved further away from growing towns.

The reserved lands were allocated to both individual families and clusters of families. The smaller blocks were revoked first, forcing people onto the larger ones. The clusters of families formed new communities and referred to the reserves as 'missions' regardless of whether they were administered by government or missionaries. The missions, as they are still called, formed the basis of the contemporary 'local Aboriginal communities' throughout New South Wales. All the revocations were illegal but were retrospectively legalised in 1983 before freehold title of the remaining lands was handed to these local Aboriginal communities. Only a quarter of the land they had been allocated was left to be transferred.

It became impossible to ignore the increasing numbers of children being born from sexual relations between settler men and Aboriginal women, unions which were both voluntary and involuntary. This negated the idea that the Aboriginal 'race' would die out, disturbing many white Australians who felt that it was inappropriate for children with 'European blood' to grow up in Aboriginal (although European controlled) environments. It was believed that these children could be assimilated into menial positions within the European hierarchy of class and status. The European practice of removing children of lower class, poor or single parents in order to use them for farm labour was already well established, and was used by the British in Canada as well.

Once the violent interactions abated, it became clear that the Aboriginal population was recovering and increasing. In 1938, a Commonwealth-wide meeting recommended a new policy of assimilation. Assimilation was a different approach to disappearance. This is what was expected would happen to Aboriginal people. Despite the often humanitarian rhetoric of colonial practice, disappearance through actual genocide or through assimilation as cultural genocide, was about the erasure of difference in white Australia.

Although colonial governments seemed unwilling or unable to put a stop to the violence against Aborigines, the British government responded more positively. As early as 1837, they set up the first of what would be several Select Committees inquiring into the treatment of Aboriginal people, recommending that they would be better defended ('protected') by a special system of laws to be administered by Protectors. The protectorate system was to attend in particular to the education of young people, aided by missionaries. Whatever the original intentions of the protectorates, they increasingly became systems of oppression. The laws of 'protection' were used over time to significantly curtail Aboriginal rights – rights that were not restored until the 1960s.

The historical context for the Apology

Assimilation as policy was first implemented in Victoria, where a 1886 Statute ruled that all 'half-castes' were to be expelled from Aboriginal reserves. Aboriginal people were thus divided into two groups, of which only one was officially regarded as Aboriginal (Beckett 1988:197–98; Wolfe 1994:101,106). This also became policy in Queensland.

In New South Wales the increase in people of mixed descent meant they would become described as 'part-Aborigines'. Arbitrary distinctions began to be made between 'full blood' and 'part-Aborigines', the latter divided into 'half-castes', 'quarter-castes' and even 'octoroons' (of eight great grandparents, one was Aboriginal). All such 'castes' were treated as Aboriginal in New South Wales' legislation.

These labels were imposed on people who were growing up as Aboriginal children with Aboriginal parents and as part of Aboriginal communities. While they may have had a white parent or grandparent, socially and culturally they were Aboriginal. The classifications were largely on the basis of skin colour, irrespective of parentage. Children with the same parents were often classified and treated differently; those with lighter skin being considered more educable and able to take a place amongst the European community (Read 1999:20–22).

Lighter-skinned children became a particular target for removal. Indigenous children could be taken from their families and communities and sent out to work for non-Indigenous people, which would eventually lead to these people being absorbed into the non-Indigenous population (HREOC 1997:29).

Initially the Aboriginal Protection Board used threats and persuasion to remove children. They also used the *Neglected Children and Juvenile Offenders Act* of 1905 to remove children they defined as neglected or uncontrollable. This act was considered inadequate by the Board because it allowed for children to be placed with extended family members, and magistrates often refused to commit Aboriginal children who seemed to be well looked after. The Board lobbied for specific legislation giving them greater control. It was granted this in 1909 in the form of the *Aborigines Protection Act* which gave them power to:

> assume full control and custody of the child of any aborigine, if after due enquiry it is satisfied that such a course was in the interest of the moral and physical welfare of the child (Read 1999:28).

It also gave the Board the right to apprentice Aboriginal children between 14 and 18 years old. In 1914, the Board ordered that all mixed descent boys over 14 years old be sent off the missions to seek employment, and all girls over 14 years old had to go into domestic service or to the Cootamundra Training Home for girls (HREOC 1997:40). In 1918, the Board established the Kinchela Training Institution for Aboriginal boys, which was moved to Kempsey in 1924. Younger children and babies were put into the United Aborigines Mission home at Bomaderry on the New South Wales south coast (HREOC 1997:31, 44).

As one of the aims of removal was to control the reproduction of Indigenous people, girls were particularly targeted for removal and domestic labour. In 1893, a girls dormitory was built on Warangesda mission, and until 1909, about 300 Aboriginal children from various areas were taken from their families and placed there (HREOC 1997:40), where they grew up with children born on the mission. In New South Wales up until 1921, about 80 percent of children removed were girls. Those figures had only decreased slightly by 1936. Girls stayed at the Cootamundra Girls Home until they were 14 years old, after which they were sent out to work as domestics. Girls who became pregnant (often as a result of being raped by their employers) had their children removed.

Up until 1915, the Board still had to prove that children were neglected under the *Neglected Children and Juvenile Offenders Act* 1905 before they could have children removed from their families. As well as experiencing problems in persuading parents to relinquish their children willingly, they often faced difficulties in the courts when attempting to remove children on the basis of neglect. They sought an amendment which would grant them the power to separate Aboriginal children from their families without a court hearing and this was legislated in 1915. The Board could then remove children for a host of reasons including simply for 'being Aboriginal' (Read 1999:30).

The Amendment also abolished the minimum age at which Aboriginal children could be apprenticed. While parents could appeal the decision to remove their children, their chances of success were negligible, resulting in many parents fleeing the stations, missions and reserves in order to protect their children (HREOC 1997:41–42). By the end of World War I, the Board had the power to remove all children under 18 years from reserves, as well as any men they felt should have been off working somewhere else, and anyone they considered to be more than 'half European' (Read 1999:30).

Another way of enforcing the separation of mixed descent Aborigines from their families and communities was through the constantly changing definition of 'Aboriginal'. Over 67 definitions have been found in over 700 pieces of legislation nation-wide (HREOC 1997:30). For example, after 1905 the New South Wales Government's illegal reclamation of land specifically gazetted for Aboriginal use, as well as the subdivision of many of the larger stations, forced many of the Aboriginal people who had lived in these places onto reserves or town fringes. The Board responded to the increased costs they accrued by changing the definition of an 'Aborigine'.

The historical context for the Apology

They ruled that those children they labelled 'quadroon' and 'octoroon' were no longer allowed to live on the reserves with their families. However, the people forced off the reserves were not accepted into the non-Aboriginal world and in 1936 the Board changed the definition of Aboriginality again in order to take control of Aboriginal children living outside the reserves and stations. People who refused the type of employment advocated by the Board could be put into institutions, and those families who refused to move onto reserves or from one reserve to another were threatened with the removal of their children. It was left to the local police to carry out the Board's removal policies, provide 'protection' to Aboriginal people, distribute rations and prosecute offenders (HREOC 1997:43).

At the national Commonwealth–State Native Welfare Conference in 1937, it was decided that:

> the destiny of the natives of aboriginal origin, but not of the full blood, lies in their ultimate absorption by the people of the Commonwealth, and it therefore recommends that all efforts be directed to that end ... [and that] efforts of all State authorities should be directed towards the education of children of mixed aboriginal blood at white standards, and their subsequent employment under the same conditions as whites with a view to their taking their place in the white community on an equal footing with the whites (HREOC 1997:32).

By 1939, there were over 180 reserves in NSW. These included 'managed reserves' known by the Board as stations and generally run by a teacher-manager. Stations provided housing, rations and some type of education. There were also unmanaged reserves on which rations were provided but no housing or education. These came under the control of local police but provided a degree of autonomy compared with the stations (HREOC 1997:40). If a reserve population grew too big, it would be turned into a managed station.

In 1940, the Board was renamed the Aborigines Welfare Board, and held responsibility for the new policy of assimilation. Children now had to be removed according to the *Child Welfare Act* 1939, based on them being considered 'neglected', 'destitute' or 'uncontrollable' by a court. Courts ordered the removal of Aboriginal children for these reasons far more readily than non-Indigenous children, and removal was more than often permanent, involving denial of access between parents and children. Aboriginal child-rearing practices, such as care by extended family members, were viewed negatively, and many Aboriginal people still camped out. Both practices were enough to declare any children involved 'neglected'.

Once they had been removed, Aboriginal children became wards of the Aborigines Welfare Board which took over from the Aboriginal Protection

One life, two stories

Board in 1940, whereas non-Aboriginal children were under the control of the Child Welfare Department. Aboriginal wards who left their employment or institution could be punished by the Children's Court, and Aboriginal parents of wards were forbidden by law to contact their children. The Welfare Board could bypass court procedures for removal by 'persuading' parents to sign over their children (HREOC 1997:47).

Overcrowding in the Aborigines Welfare Board's institutions led to new arrangements. From 1942, Aboriginal children ruled 'uncontrollable' by the Children's Court were made the responsibility of the Child Welfare Department. In general, they would then be sent to Corrective Institutions such as the Parramatta Girls Home or, in the case of boys, Mount Penang. During the 1940s and 1950s, the Child Welfare Department and Aborigines Welfare Board worked together in placing Aboriginal children, often according to skin colour. Lighter-skinned children were sent to non-Aboriginal institutions or placed in non-Aboriginal foster homes.

During the 1950s and 1960s, increasing numbers of Aboriginal children were removed. This was designed to speed up the process of assimilation. It led to a problem of overcrowded institutions. A movement against the institutionalisation of children led to foster homes coming to be regarded as the ideal means to assimilate Aboriginal children into the white community. In 1950, the Board placed advertisements for foster parents for 150 Aboriginal children. By 1958, 116 wards had been fostered, 90 with non-Aboriginal families. In 1960, more than 300 Aboriginal children were in foster homes, with over 70 in Cootamundra and Kinchela.

Aboriginal children were also adopted out, their mothers often being coerced into signing adoption papers either just after they had given birth or after their children had already been forcibly removed. In New South Wales, the Aborigines Welfare Board was unable to consent to the adoption of its wards. However, under the *Adoption of Children Act* 1965, when a foster parent wished to adopt a ward of the Board, the Board could bypass the child's family by applying to the Children's Court to waive the consent requirement if they regarded the mother unfit to be a parent or guardian (HREOC 1997:34, 48–49).

By the early 1960s, it was evident that Aboriginal people were not being assimilated as planned. Not only did discrimination mean that non-Aboriginal people did not wish to assimilate them, Aboriginal people themselves were not willing to give up their own lifestyles and cultural practices. Their worlds had changed significantly over time in response to the constraints and pressures of their colonial experiences. Nevertheless, they were worlds in which they had reconstituted distinct and meaningful *Aboriginal* lives for themselves.

The historical context for the Apology

The official definition of assimilation was changed in the 1960s to incorporate the idea that Aboriginal people should be able to choose to live like other Australians (HREOC 1997:34–35). Real change started to happen after 1967 when a Constitutional Referendum gave the Commonwealth Government power for the first time to legislate in respect of Aboriginal people. A Federal Office of Aboriginal Affairs was established and grants made available to set up social programs of various kinds. In 1969, the policy of assimilation was officially changed to one of integration.

The NSW Aborigines Welfare Board was abolished in 1969 but this did not end the removals. The Board's wards were transferred to the Department for Child Welfare and Social Welfare, and Kinchela and Cootamundra Homes closed shortly after. However, the Bomaderry home was in operation until 1980. The closure of these homes simply meant that Aboriginal children who rebelled against their removal or their foster homes were sent to a detention centre (HREOC 1997:49–50).

After 1972, under the Whitlam Government's policy of Aboriginal self-determination, Aboriginal groups were able to obtain funding to counter the high rates of child removal. The Aboriginal Children's Service was set up in Sydney by the same group of Aboriginal people who had lobbied successfully for the establishment of the Aboriginal Legal Service. It focussed its work on insisting that Aboriginal children who did require guardianship be cared for by Aboriginal rather than non-Aboriginal people, and by ensuring that Aboriginal children were represented in court. The intervention of the Aboriginal Legal Service in child removal cases led to an immediate decrease in the numbers of children removed, as well as placement with Aboriginal families for those who were.

The discrimination inherent in child removal policies, as well as that which was faced by Aboriginal children growing up in non-Aboriginal environments, was eventually brought to public attention in the late 1970s. This led to changes in the policies for the removal and placement of Aboriginal children through the 1980s.

Although these early Aboriginal-run organisations did eventually receive regular funding, the Aboriginal Children's Service in particular was poorly supported and its committed staff often went without wages over the first two decades. Another voluntary organisation which later received funding was Link Up, set up in 1980, also in New South Wales. This group wanted to help Aboriginal people trying to trace their children, or children to trace their families. They organised many reunions of families who had suffered under child removal policies and practices (HREOC, 1997:36). Link Up is now a national organisation.

From the mid 1970s, the NSW Department of Youth and Community Services started to involve Aboriginal workers in the placement of Aboriginal children. By 1978, the Department employed 12 Aboriginal caseworkers. In 1985–86, Departmental policies regarding adoption and fostering were developed which recognised that Aboriginal children needing to be removed should be placed with Aboriginal families whenever possible. Within a year this led to a 12 percent reduction of the number of Aboriginal wards. *The Children (Care and Protection) Act* 1987 incorporated the Aboriginal Child Placement Principle, whereby Aboriginal families were the preferred option for Aboriginal children needing care (HREOC 1997:50–51). Amendments to the *Adoption Act* in 1990 also recognised that cultural values regarding care of children by extended family members should be taken into account.

The Stolen Generations

Peter Read is a historian who carried out extensive research with and about Aboriginal people who were separated from their families as a result of various government policies and practices implemented over the last two centuries. He was a co-founder of Link Up. In his article, 'A rape of the soul so profound' (1999), Read explains that the term 'Stolen Generation' was meant to encompass the range of people who were affected by these practices in different ways. He stressed that the underlying common denominator was, as one person had put it:

> We Stolen Generations are the victims of Australia-wide policies which aimed to separate us from our parents, our family, our neighbourhood, our community, our country and our rightful inheritance as Aboriginal citizens of Australia (Read 1999:xi).

Aboriginal children removed from their families and raised away from their communities in institutions or non-Aboriginal homes were subjected to attitudes and practices based on an understanding of Aboriginality as something of no social worth. Children living in institutions were rarely, if ever, allowed to meet with their parents and were not taught anything about their Aboriginality except that it was something inferior, of which they should be ashamed. Many children who lived in these institutions report how lonely and unloved they felt. Large numbers attempted to run away, often repeatedly. They received little education that would equip them for anything except a life of servitude (Read 1999:33–36).

Children who were fostered or adopted out faced both similar and different problems. Even those who were loved by their new families often grew up without any sense of their Aboriginality. It was common for children not to be told they were of Aboriginal descent but rather Polynesian, Indian or some other more acceptable background. Anglo-Australian adoptive or foster parents were rarely equipped to provide children in their care with the means to counter racism or to develop a sense of pride in their Aboriginal identity (Read 1999:37–39) given that pejorative attitudes to Aboriginal people permeated Australian life. At least those in the institutions had some shared experience of Aboriginality, however negative, and consequently could learn a resilience which helped them in later life.

While the practice of removing children was widespread throughout Australia, a variety of laws and policies over time led to varying degrees of intensity in removal practices. A lack of comprehensive historical records has made it difficult to formulate accurate statistics regarding the extent of child removals. There are estimates that as many as 100,000 people of Aboriginal descent alive today may still not know their families or communities. Many may not even be aware that they are of Aboriginal descent (Edwards and Read 1989:ix).

There are a number of prominent Australians, including Federal politicians, who have asserted that the removals of Aboriginal children were the result of 'well-intentioned', even if misguided, policies and that these were policies similar to those under which non-Aboriginal children were also removed. Such 'good intentions' are still being used as an ideological justification for not compensating those affected. One hears the argument that it is totally inappropriate to refer to the practice of removal as 'genocide'. This public rejection of genocide is in response to the claim that, under United Nations' charters, to forcibly deny people access to their rightful cultural heritage is 'cultural genocide' and that removal of Aboriginal children clearly had this intent in a great many, if not a majority of cases.

Aboriginal children were treated differently to non-Aboriginal children. For instance, they were often denied information about their kin, even when as adults they left the homes and institutions they had been assigned to. Historical evidence clearly shows that Aboriginal children were removed as part of racially based programs of cultural genocide. In the mid twentieth century, eugenics theories propagated the belief that 'Aboriginal blood' could be diluted and that Aboriginal people could thus eventually be absorbed or assimilated into European society. This was considered a humanitarian solution to 'the half-caste problem' (see, for instance, Neville 1940). If the so-called half-caste children were segregated from their families and communities, and if their marriages were carefully controlled, it was hoped descendants would become 'whiter' with each generation (Neville 1940:54).

Reconciliation

In 1991, the Commonwealth Parliament voted unanimously to set up the Council for Aboriginal Reconciliation (CAR), establishing a formal process for reconciliation to take place over the decade leading up to 2001 (Huggins 2001:5–6), the centenary of Australia's federation.

One life, two stories

Paul Keating, then Prime Minister, in his famous Redfern Park speech in 1992, acknowledged the crimes and injustices inflicted by white Australians on Aboriginal people. His declaration was a long awaited call by Indigenous Australian's for the nation's recognition of the injustices suffered by Indigenous people.

> It was we who did the dispossessing. We took the traditional lands and smashed the traditional way of life; we brought the diseases, the alcohol; we committed the murders; we took the children from their mothers; we practiced discrimination and exclusion. It was our ignorance and prejudice, and our failure to imagine these things being done to us. With some noble exceptions, we failed to make the most basic human response and enter into their hearts and minds. We failed to ask: 'How would I feel if this were done to me?'
> (www.antar.org.au/issues_and_campaigns/self-determination/paul_keating_redfern_speech)

Keating's speech constituted an act of bearing witness, a call for all Australians to subjectively engage with the traumas of history and acknowledge their (our) implication in the repercussions of the crimes enacted. In 2007, Radio National listeners voted Keating's speech third in a list of world history's most unforgettable speeches.

In May 1995, the Keating Government set up the National Inquiry into the Separation of Aboriginal and Torres Strait Islander Children from Their Families. The Inquiry was carried out by the Human Rights and Equal Opportunity Commission (HREOC). In 1996, the Keating Labor government lost office and the Howard Liberal–National Coalition was elected. The report from the National Inquiry, the *Bringing Them Home* report was released in May 1997.

The newly appointed Minister for Aboriginal and Torres Strait Islander Affairs, Senator John Herron responded to the ongoing work of the Inquiry in 1996 by stating, 'What we must recognise is that a lot of people have benefited by that [policy of removal]' (*The Weekend Australian*, 5 October 1996:3). His response was reportedly based on a conversation with an Aboriginal woman who told him that she had received the benefit of an education as a result of being removed. He also claimed that the then Chair of ATSIC, (the Aboriginal and Torres Strait Islander Commission which operated from 1990 until 2005), Lois Lowitja O'Donoghue, who was removed from her family when she was two years old, shared this opinion. However, O'Donoghue immediately refuted his claim, stressing that benefits such as education could in no way make up for the irretrievable loss of family, culture and language that removal entailed. Herron's claim

The historical context for the Apology

glosses over the historical fact that a majority of Aboriginal children were often denied access to adequate education unless they had been removed – and many of those did not receive it even after their removal. The lack of opportunity that resulted from such limited access to education is a direct consequence of policies of exclusion.

Senator Herron also questioned the benefits of financial compensation and the provision of funding for counselling services for people who experienced removal, asserting 'What's done cannot be undone' (*Sydney Morning Herald*, 10 October 1996:9). He argued that 'a great deal of benefit will occur just purely out of the process of people being able to go before that inquiry and talking about what has happened to them' (*Weekend Australian*, 5 October 1996:3). This comment does not distinguish between the 'telling' of the story and most importantly, having one's voice heard by an addressable other, by a person prepared to bear witness to the trauma being recounted.

While Senator Herron's comment might sound like recognition of the positive role of the Inquiry, his denial of the necessity of an adequate and appropriate response to the Inquiry's findings constituted a refusal to acknowledge the crucial importance of these findings for the future development of policy. Neither Senator Herron, nor Prime Minister Howard appeared to have considered the effects of having one's stories of removal fall on deaf ears to those who, often with great difficulty, had come forward to testify to their trauma.

Even before the Inquiry published its report and recommendations in 1997, John Howard, then Prime Minister, expressed his doubts about its 'long term value and practical contribution' (*Sydney Morning Herald* , 17 October 1996:6), demonstrating his lack of understanding of the Inquiry as providing a means for people to tell their stories and to have them properly listened to. Howard claimed his response was based on concern about claims for monetary compensation that may have resulted from the Inquiry.

However, Mick Dodson, the Aboriginal and Torres Strait Islander Social Justice Commissioner at that time, pointed out that an overwhelming majority of people who had told their stories to the Inquiry did not bring up the issue of monetary compensation. Rather they were primarily concerned with receiving 'an acknowledgment of what happened, an explanation of why it happened to them and an apology' (*The Australian*, 11 October 1996:11). In other words, they wanted Australians to bear witness to their painful journeys. What was being sought was a witness who would make an appropriate response.

At the time of the Report's release in May 1997, the Australian Reconciliation Convention was being held in Melbourne. Mick Dodson and Sir Ron Witton, HREOC Commissioners on the Inquiry, organised to launch the Report at the Convention. The issue of the removal of Indigenous children from their families and communities was on everybody's minds and the Convention provided the opportunity for many speakers to express their feelings about these tragic events. The Inquiry estimated that between 10 and 30 percent of all Indigenous children were forcibly removed from their families and communities between 1910 and 1970. Pat Dodson requested a one minute silence for the stolen children before he spoke about reconciliation (McRae, Nettheim, Beacroft and McNamara 2003).

One of the pivotal recommendations of the Inquiry's final Report was the need for an official national apology to those individuals and families who had been affected by past policies of removal. This was considered an essential part of the reconciliation process between Indigenous and non-Indigenous Australians.

Cheryl Kernot, then Leader of the Democrats in the Federal Parliament, immediately apologised for past government practices of 'stealing children from their families', and gave recognition to the fact that apologies were about healing and forgiveness (*The Australian*, 27 May 1997:1). Many other sectors of the Australian community, including State governments, made formal apologies at that time and demonstrated their support for a national apology. In June 1997, the New South Wales Government made a formal statement of apology. Nancy de Vries was asked to receive this apology on behalf of the people who had been removed in this State. Her acceptance speech and the apology from the Carr Labor government are reproduced at the beginning of this book.

However, the response of the Federal Government was very disappointing. John Howard, as Prime Minister, refused to apologise on behalf of the Federal Government on the grounds that an official apology would implicate present generations for the actions of previous generations which were sanctioned by law and believed at the time to be in the best interests of the children involved. He did grudgingly provide a personal apology, on 26 May 1997 at the Australian Reconciliation Convention in Melbourne. He identified the practice of child removal as 'a most blemished chapter' of Australia's history and said that as a nation we need to acknowledge the injustices done. He stated:

> Personally I feel deep sorrow for those of my fellow Australians who suffered injustices under the practices of past generations of Australian people. Equally, I am sorry for the hurt and trauma many here today continue to feel as a consequence of those practices (CAR 1997).

His 'apology' was not specifically addressed to the Stolen Generations and he specified that it was a personal statement rather than a statement on

The historical context for the Apology

behalf of the Australian nation and its people. The disappointed audience's response was hostile. The audience simply stood up and turned their backs on the Prime Minister. His response was widely considered inadequate.

Mr Howard's refusal to make an official apology was based on his claim that to do so would imply the guilt and responsibility of present generations of Australians who had nothing to do with the forced removals. This was in spite of the fact that the recommendation for a national apology refuted such implications.

In December 1997, Senator Herron, Federal Minister for Aboriginal and Torres Strait Islander Affairs, presented the Federal Government's formal response to the HREOC Report to Parliament. This response was also considered to be inadequate by Indigenous people and various organisations. Abrahams (1998:15) for instance pointed out in the *Indigenous Law Bulletin* that the response did not include an official government apology, did not deal with two-thirds of the Report's recommendations, and that the funds allocated were totally inadequate to bring about the necessary changes. She made the point that the act of apologising to the Stolen Generations for the damage done to them, by formally acknowledging their suffering, 'is an essential element of their healing process'. She stated that 'the provision of practical measures to alleviate the effects of the harm ... can have no lasting impact' without it, as 'an apology gives validity and strength to any subsequent practical acts'.

In his 2000 submission to a Senate Committee on the Stolen Generations (Herron 2000), Senator Herron focussed on what he saw as problems with the HREOC report. He contested the research findings of the Report. First he contested the estimated number of Indigenous children removed under past government policies and practices as cited in the Report, and second the use of the term 'generation' to speak of those children removed. He expressed the Federal Government's concern 'that there is no reliable basis for what appears to be a generally accepted conclusion as to the supposed dimensions of the "stolen generation"'. He quibbled with the figures cited, branding them 'inflated' – the result of 'uncertain guesstimates and shoddy research' (Herron 2000). His submission was largely concerned with the issue of numbers and he emphasised the Government's position that the removal of Indigenous children was not always forced or negative.

In pressing his point, Senator Herron paired every recognition of the *negatives* of removal and the circumstances surrounding such removal with a *positive*: the reasons for removal were 'good or bad', 'protective and otherwise'; the removals themselves occurred 'forcibly or with consent', 'voluntarily or involuntarily', 'legitimate or otherwise', 'forcibly or otherwise', 'some forcibly and some not'. He spoke of 'situations which could not be accurately described as "stolen children" or even "forcible removal" – for example, children who were orphaned, genuinely surrendered for adoption, fostered out by their own parents, or statutorily removed for their own protection, whether for reasons of neglect or worse.'

The statements made in this submission indicated that Senator Herron had not read the evidence, for instance, concerning the manner in which Indigenous mothers were coerced into 'allowing' their children to be fostered or adopted out – or the extreme powerlessness experienced by those who were not only young and female but also Indigenous.

Senator Herron seemed unaware just how various laws were created and amended to facilitate the removal of Indigenous children 'for their own protection', or how easy it was to claim 'neglect' in order that the government could implement its prime aim of separating Indigenous children from their families and communities by whatever means necessary. Neglect could mean little more than being poor or not having adequate housing. In the light of such evidence, Herron's protestations were clearly baseless.

However, the fact that many people reading Herron's submission would have been unaware of the background of the Stolen Generations and would be unlikely to read the HREOC Report, meant that it was all too easy to get the public caught up in the issues around 'appropriate' estimates of numbers of children and semantics, rather than to take on board for themselves the substance of the report, the horrendous stories and truths revealed.

Herron concluded his submission by denying the possibility that the removal of Indigenous children affected 'vast numbers', or that it resulted in 'whole generations of trauma across the entire indigenous community'. He declared the term 'stolen generation' rhetorical. In this way he denied due recognition of the trauma of removal as experienced by so many Indigenous Australians.

The most public achievements of the Decade of Reconciliation were the Reconciliation Walks. In the last six months of 2000 at least one million people all over Australia walked over bridges in cities and country towns in a symbolic gesture of reconciliation. The biggest of these was the Walk for Reconciliation over the Sydney Harbour Bridge. More than 250,000 people walked across the Bridge, including Nancy and her grandchildren.

A granting of compensation could have constituted a gesture of acknowledgment and apology – although it could also have been construed as an attempt to silence those Aboriginal people who continue to speak out about the injustices of removal and its ongoing consequences. But a gesture of compensation would undoubtedly have signified the government's recognition of its own role and responsibility. Fundamentally, it was this recognition which continued to be refused and was evident in associated debates, such as the refusal to acknowledge the magnitude of Aboriginal deaths in the conflicts on the colonial frontier and other aspects of colonial

The historical context for the Apology

history, contestations which have come to be known in Australia as the 'history wars'. Such debates are part of a long-standing and widespread refusal to acknowledge the Aboriginal presence. The impact of this refusal extends far beyond the removal of children and even the frontier death rate.

It was not until 2007, when the Howard Liberal National Coalition Government was defeated by Kevin Rudd's Labor Government that cynicism at the Federal level was reversed. Rudd made good on his pre-election promise that the Government would say sorry. After months of consultation, he delivered The Apology on 13 February 2008, in which he said:

> To the Stolen Generations, I say the following: as Prime Minister of Australia, I am sorry. On behalf of the government of Australia, I am sorry. On behalf of the parliament of Australia, I am sorry. I offer you this apology without qualification. We apologise for the hurt, the pain and suffering that we, the parliament, have caused you by the laws that previous parliaments have enacted. We apologise for the indignity, the degradation and the humiliation these laws embodied. We offer this apology to the mothers, the fathers, the brothers, the sisters, the families and the communities whose lives were ripped apart by the actions of successive governments under successive parliaments.

In his speech, he bore witness to the testimony of one member of the Stolen Generations, Nanna Nungala Fejo, after which he emphasised:

> Nanna Fejo's is just one story. There are thousands, tens of thousands, of them: stories of forced separation of Aboriginal and Torres Strait Islander children from their mums and dads over the better part of a century. Some of these stories are graphically told in *Bringing them home*, the report commissioned in 1995 by Prime Minister Keating and received in 1997 by Prime Minister Howard. There is something terribly primal about these firsthand accounts. The pain is searing; it screams from the pages. The hurt, the humiliation, the degradation and the sheer brutality of the act of physically separating a mother from her children is a deep assault on our senses and on our most elemental humanity.
>
> These stories cry out to be heard; they cry out for an apology. Instead, from the nation's parliament there has been a stony and stubborn and deafening silence for more than a decade. (Rudd 2008)

However, while acknowledging the importance of bearing witness, Rudd also ruled out financial compensation for people who experienced removal.

One life, two stories

While Indigenous leaders welcomed the apology, they said the question of compensation would still need to be considered.

Removal narratives

The production of the HREOC Report provided a great many Aboriginal and Torres Strait Islander people with the opportunity to share their experiences of trauma, and many stories of removal were published during and after the Report was produced, in associated publications, educational literature, information brochures, academic texts and official reports, as well as through autobiographical, biographical, and fictional forms, and on radio, television and film.

However, there continued to be inadequate response to these narratives of removal. The lack of recognition at the Federal level, by the Howard Coalition government, overshadowed the considerable efforts made by State and Local Governments, other public and private institutions (professional associations, churches, armed and police forces) and members of the public to more effectively respond to the issue of removal and its ongoing effects.

This was to some extent remedied by Rudd's apology in 2007. However, despite the cathartic impact of Rudd's apology, removal narratives remain important and will continue to be so until Australia as a nation has reconciled itself to its history.

Why are these stories significant? What constitutes an 'appropriate' response – from the state and from individuals? Although they might all be called removal narratives, they are very diverse and none are 'typical'. But that is not the only reason to keep telling them. The continual need to tell these stories and to keep these issues on the public agenda has been necessitated by a paucity of appropriate responses to them.

Public debates continue to express, on the one hand, a defensive, even offensive, tone and, on the other, frustration, hurt and anger. Public responses could be divided into two categories: those which reflect an identification with and recognition of the trauma of removal, thus acknowledge the importance of these stories being told and heard; and those which, often drawing on 'facts' and statistical information as evidence, claim a greater access to the 'truth' of removal than the Aboriginal people who experienced it.

The histories of Aboriginal people caught up within the project of building the Australian nation-state have proved too confronting. As a consequence, Australia continues to live in a state of crisis in which, as a nation, it resists confrontation.

Aboriginal historian Jackie Huggins (2001:5–6) stresses that an understanding of 'the tragic history of Aboriginal child removal ... and what

The historical context for the Apology

this episode signifies for both Indigenous and other Australians' is essential to the achievement of reconciliation.

To deny history is to deny recognition to the people who have lived that history. This applies as much to the history of a people as it does to any one person: the denial implies they do not matter. Aboriginal peoples' experiences during the colonial years of founding and developing the nation state as we know it today were denied in Australia for a very long time. They began to be included in the national history only from the late 1970s. But resistance on the part of some non-Indigenous Australians to the incorporation of the stories of these colonised peoples within the Australian story persists.

The introduction into Australian history of stories of cruel and insensitive policies and practices which split families asunder has proved particularly difficult. The reasons are complex but in this context undoubtedly one is because 'the family', 'mothering' and 'children' are expected within Australian value systems to be sites for nurturance and protection, a focus for state support. It is not legitimate to separate families without good reason – and 'being Aboriginal' is not a good reason. Another reason for the resistance is because, as these stories of child removal surfaced, it became clear that the dark side of Australia's past remained a very real part of the nation's present – which continues to demand a response, both personal and political. This is not only in relation to child removals but the whole experience of colonial violence and subjugation, as this has played out through a formerly sanitised Australian national history and rhetoric.

'Too loud not to hear': Responding to stories of removal

The haunting echoes of the cries of our stolen children is too loud not to hear; the physical and emotional effects of this human calamity too visible not to see; the violation we feel as a community too real not to voice. ... White Australia failed, the Prime Minister [Paul Keating] said, to make the most basic human response and enter into the hearts and minds of the Aboriginal people. Yet, like the Prime Minister, we do not believe that this report, nor others that have come before it, should fill the wider community with guilt. It should instead prompt that community to open its heart and listen to what our people are saying (ALS WA, *Telling our story,* 1995:iv–v).

Telling Nancy's story

This book was a cooperative effort. It is both an autobiography – Nancy's story told by Nancy herself – and a biography, in that Jane, Gaynor and Anna helped gather and shape that story with Nancy. As Nancy's co-writers, we wanted to situate her story in ways that assist you, our reader, to understand that telling such a story is not a simple task. We also invite you, our readers, to reflect on what it means to hear a person telling her story of a life lived with injury and trauma. We share with you what it has meant for us to be a part of the telling of Nancy's story – and what we have learnt about bearing witness to that story.

There are different stories in this book. Most importantly, there is Nancy's own story. Nancy also shares with us her discovery of the story told about her as a child, according to the files of the Child Welfare Department, Nancy's official guardian. It makes a painful contrast.

This book also tells about a period in Australia's story, about the kind of nation it has been and is becoming – it explores attitudes, practices, policies and processes which impacted daily on Nancy's life but of which, as a child, she was unaware. As you have already read, removal narratives have been a confronting part of Australia's history.

The narrative of this book isn't always neat. Lives and 'truths' don't come in neat packages. There are contradictions in accounts and plenty of 'gaps'. That is how it was for Nancy. The story leaves many questions unanswered. Some are unanswerable, some do not require answers and others need a great deal more reflection, on our part and on yours.

Bearing witness

Nancy's story is a 'removal narrative', one of the thousands of stories Aboriginal and Torres Strait Islander people have to tell of their experience of being taken from their families. Removal narratives, despite their differences, and whether they have been produced orally in the presence of a listener or in more literary forms, are 'testimonies'. They testify to the arbitrary, misguided and frequently contemptible nature of non-Aboriginal perceptions and treatment of Aboriginal people in the past and the present. They testify to unacknowledged crimes committed by non-Aboriginal people against Aboriginal people and to the enduring nature of the wounds that were inflicted. They testify to the existence of Aboriginal identities which have emerged as a result of, in resistance to, and in spite of past policies and practices aimed at eliminating the possibility of such identities (if not aimed at eliminating Aboriginal people altogether). Removal narratives are testimonies of trauma.

Aboriginal removal narratives are 'testimonies' in the sense that their production is dependent on the presence of a 'witness' or 'witnesses', even if this witness is imaginary or implied, as in the case of written forms. You, the reader, are a witness at this moment. As co-authors we were called upon to be witnesses in writing this book with Nancy. The role of the witness is more complex than one of spectator, observer or reader. It means to become 'an addressable other'. Aboriginal people telling their own narratives of removal need a response that will grant recognition and facilitate healing for those who feel able to speak as well as those who prefer to remain silent. As Laub (1992:68) says of trauma victims:

> The absence of an empathic listener, or more radically, the absence of an addressable other, an other who can hear the anguish of one's memories and thus affirm and recognise their realness, annihilates the story.
>
> Without a witness or an appropriate response, there is no acknowledgment of the trauma of the past, or its reverberations in the present. The story – and the person who is the story – is annihilated. The trauma is intensified.

There has been resistance on the part of many non-Aboriginal Australians to becoming this type of 'witness', this 'addressable other'. This was evident in the defensive nature of responses to the Inquiry, to public debates that have appeared in major newspapers, and even to films that

'Too loud not to hear'

Nancy visiting Willoughby Public School, where she was once a pupil herself, during National Aborigines and Islanders week in July 2000, sharing her story with a new generation of young Australians: 'it must never happen again.' Photographer unknown.

gained international acclaim such as *Rabbit Proof Fence.* It was evident in the reluctance of the past Howard Government to make an official statement of apology – to say 'Sorry'.

The 'witness' is initially the one who sees or experiences something. In the case of the removal of Aboriginal children, the people who experienced the trauma of removal are the initial witnesses. These are the children themselves, their mothers, fathers, brothers and sisters, aunts and uncles – that whole network of relations that make up every Aboriginal person's social world. No one is left untouched by the removal of a child from their midst. Aboriginal people were seldom able to testify to their traumatic experiences at the time they occurred. They have had to bear the burden of their witnessing, often alone and over many years.

When there is the opportunity of speaking out, the one who is addressed also becomes a witness to the trauma of the person to whom they are listening. Sometimes it can be unbearable to be a witness. Stories can be and often are heartbreaking. Aboriginal people can find it painful to speak out, even among their own families. But once a person is prepared to become a witness – not just a listener – he or she then feels compelled to enable the story he or she has heard to reach a wider audience – to find people who will bear witness to his or her own experience of having become a witness, someone who now shares some of that pain. Just as we are doing through this book.

An event without a witness

Because removal has had such a profound effect on the lives of so many, it is now an issue increasingly discussed in a variety of public and private arenas. Australians now have opportunities to bear witness to Aboriginal testimonies of trauma. Professor Beverley Raphael, the Director of Mental Health for the NSW Health Department from 1996–2005, and an international expert on trauma and grief, first became aware of the impacts of removal in 1994, in the context of a study commissioned by the Government into Indigenous mental health. She commented, 'I was shocked that I didn't realise the extent of the separation and the trauma and grief experienced by Aboriginal people' (Mike Steketee, *Weekend Australian*, 12 October 1996:9). It is not surprising that so few non-Aboriginal people are aware of the trauma of removal when even someone in Raphael's position managed to stay in the dark for so long. Commenting on this lack of recognition, Raphael stated:

> If there is a child taken away from a parent, it is a massive news event. Yet here we have generations of children taken away from both their parents and people are wanting to deny the reality but, perhaps more importantly, the ongoing impact (*Weekend Australian*, 12 October 1996:9).

So what has been done to break the silence of the trauma of removal? The HREOC Inquiry, had it been appropriately received and responded to, could have made a great contribution to addressing the widespread ignorance of non-Aboriginal Australians regarding the extent of removal practices and their far-reaching impacts. It specifically invited Aboriginal and Torres Strait Islander people all over Australia to tell their stories. However, while it did provide many with their first opportunity to testify to their removal experiences before a witness, many people's removal experiences were so traumatic that they remain unable or unwilling to speak about them (see Read 1995:22). There may be reasons other than trauma itself which dissuade people who were removed from coming forward.

The tremendous number of testimonies of trauma that have been produced is mind-numbingly distressing. Their combined effect is a litany of loss, grief, pain, fear, anger, confusion, abuse, crises, deprivation,

'Too loud not to hear'

degradation and more. Few removal narratives are free of pain. Some people may not regard their experiences as traumatic. Some people who have experienced trauma may feel that others would not see their experiences as worthy of note. The issue of what constitutes trauma is complex. It is not something easily measured. But even people adopted into loving families, who speak positively of many of their post-removal experiences, also speak of a sense of irretrievable loss, feelings of identity crisis, or feelings of not knowing where or to whom they belong(ed).

While speaking out is understood as a means of facilitating healing for those whose removal experiences were traumatic, this is not the only thing that compels people to speak. The Inquiry, along with other associated initiatives, motivated people to narrate their experiences. Establishing the Inquiry, and its official context, offered hope that something could and would be done by non-Aboriginal Australians to acknowledge these overlooked aspects of Aboriginal experience and to recognise those most adversely affected. The desired result would have been a response which would have addressed and redressed the devastating implications that removal has had for individuals and communities. The required response was one which would ensure that future generations of Aboriginal people are not subjected to the dislocation and trauma that past policies have so often entailed.

Under the Inquiry's Terms of Reference, it was required that removal narratives (along with narratives and information provided by other individuals, agencies and organisations) be assessed for the evidence they provided of the 'truth' of the affects and effects of past removal policies and practices. However, removal narratives do not, in and of themselves, speak a 'truth'. As testimonies, they constitute a 'process' through which a specific kind of 'truth' is produced.

What is the significance of Aboriginal testimonies of removal? How are the 'truths' they generate ratified or undermined by the kinds of responses they engender? The witness to these testimonies plays a crucial role: the notion of testimony centres around the particular relation between the speaking subject and the witness's response.

Because so many Aboriginal people in Australia have been subjected to either the reality or the threat of removal, removal has been what Laub (1992:80) calls 'an event without a witness'. These Aboriginal people are essentially 'insiders'. There was little possibility that there could have existed neutral 'outside' witnesses to the trauma of removal because the dehumanising colonial construction and treatment of Aboriginal people as inferior others was so widely accepted as 'truth'.

Consequently, the importance of endeavours such as Link Up, the Western Australian Aboriginal Legal Service project Telling Our Story, the Inquiry and efforts now made each May to commemorate 'Sorry Day' and Reconciliation Week should not be underestimated. These processes provide the 'addressable other' which enables the possibility of being heard.

Can we, after the Federal Government's apology, believe that the removal of Aboriginal children from their families has been unequivocally condemned as an atrocity in Australia? The aftermath of Nancy's story suggests not. Removal policies and practices are still being publicly defended or explained away. Those who become direct witnesses to removal testimonies are concerned with remedying this situation, and many of these are Aboriginal people and may have experienced removal themselves. However, those who testify are no doubt aware that in any public audience there are people who, because they appear to share the attitudes of the perpetrators and supporters of removal practices, might as well be those same people. In this sense, Aboriginal people may also be testifying (necessarily and impossibly) to their oppressors.

Those who managed to survive the death toll wrought by disease and massacre in the colonisation of their territories died before they got the opportunity to bear witness, by testifying, to the traumatic experiences they had lived through. It took a long time before their descendents could create the circumstances within which they could be heard. It is Aboriginal people themselves who now insist on the necessity of testifying and on their right to an appropriate response. Aboriginal author, Ruby Langford Ginibi, commenting on the 'revolution of Aboriginal writing', declared: 'We're all saying the same thing. Their stories, our stories that we write, they are our histories. They are our reclaiming of territory, and culture and identity'. At the same time, Archie Weller affirmed the importance of Aboriginal writers using literature as a means of pursuing, of writing, their identities (*The Australian*, 3 October 1996:5). A majority of removal narratives deal with identity as a problematic issue: experiences of trauma can radically impede or displace a trauma survivor's sense of identity. The telling of one's story to an addressable other is one means of (re)claiming one's identity.

This process of 'writing identity' does not, of course, impact solely on Aboriginal people. The transferring of these narratives into the public arena, if they are appropriately recognised and responded to, has important ramifications for non-Aboriginal people and for relations between Aboriginal and non-Aboriginal people in Australia more generally. The trauma of history, and history as trauma, affects us all. Catherine Hall (1996:66) points out when discussing African-American writer Toni Morrison's work on the importance of recovering painful historical memories, 'If such memories are not "re-membered", then they will haunt the social imagination and disrupt the present'. It is only through 're-memory' (Morrison 1988) that societies can come to terms with the racism of colonial history and its disturbing and ongoing effects.

'Too loud not to hear'

This 're-membering' of 'forgotten' aspects of Australia's history is vital if Australians wish to come to terms with the shame of a past which continues into the present. Former Prime Minister Howard's assertion that he took a 'more optimistic view of our past' *(Sydney Morning Herald* 26 October 1996:6) than that evident in histories acknowledging the racist foundations of the nation reflects a lack of recognition of the impact of this history on present generations of Australians. He was not alone and others have also spoken out against so-called 'black armband' views of Australian history. But, as Mudrooroo (1990:25) writes:

> The past is still with us. Survivors are still living, and I think that the awfulness of man's inhumanity to man should be dealt with until it becomes accepted as part of official Australian history. It is only then that Australia may free itself of its blood debt and the festering wounds of discontent.

What he is saying, as are so many others in different ways, is that Australians need to bear witness to this history – and its manifestations in the lives of individuals. They, as individuals and as a nation, need to become an addressable other.

In his review of literature on the stolen generations, Peter Read (1995:23) states that, until the 1970s, the few published Aboriginal recollections of institutional life tended to be nostalgic, possibly reflecting what non-Aboriginal people wanted to read at the time. He ascribes the emergence of Aboriginal autobiographies more critical of removal experiences to a new awareness on the part of Aboriginal people themselves that removal had resulted 'from state policies rather than their parents' shortcomings'.

Nancy's history demonstrates this well. Nancy herself was never convinced that her mother would have willingly given her up or that her mother was in some way a 'bad' mother, undeserving of her own child. This belief, which sustained her as a lonely child, was eventually vindicated when she was able to learn more about her mother and the siblings she had not grown up with.

Again and again as we worked together on this book, Nancy reminded us that she was writing this story first and foremost for her own grandchildren. So they would know and understand. They too would need to learn what it meant to bear witness to their grandmother's story. And Nancy, as she shared with us, knew only too well what it meant to have members of one's own family unable to become an addressable other with whom to share one's pain.

Nancy's focus on her vivacious grandchildren was not just so they would know more about their 'Nan'. It was also about making sure that these children could never be taken from each other or from their own cultural world. She had no confidence that 'the system' would not continue to undermine Aboriginal people and Aboriginal parenting. Her fears were well-grounded. Aboriginal children are over-represented in juvenile detention, and too many are being fostered. We might have once said mostly by Aboriginal foster parents, but this too is changing. These are symptoms of Aboriginal families still living under significant economic and social stress, still marginalised, still fighting for a recognition that does not stigmatise them in their own country.

Testimony cannot undo the trauma. It cannot return the survivor to a (real or imagined) state in which the trauma did not occur. But it can enable the survivor to explore and reconcile the differences between the 'lost' reality and the reality of their current situation. This is very different to a statement made by former Senator Herron, that we can't undo the things that have been done in the past (*Sydney Morning Herald,* 10 October 1996:9). This comment suggests that the past can and should be swept under the carpet, that people should 'move on'. To bear witness to the past is to do the opposite – to bring the past into a shared space where healing can start.

While some healing is possible when a person who has been through trauma finds an addressable other who will bear witness to their experience, it is very different when that other refuses recognition. The denial of recognition of the trauma of removal is fundamentally a denial of recognition of those who experienced that trauma, and a denial of their 'becoming' as trauma survivors. It is a denial of them as persons – a new violence to be dealt with. This is why a national apology became important to Aboriginal people – it had to be the starting point.

In relation to becoming a witness to written testimonies of trauma, Felman (1993) has recognised that some people read defensively. They do so to protect themselves from the 'risk' of the unknowable outcome and consequences of responding, of allowing the necessary 'becoming' of the other and the self in relation to the other. Reading (or listening) involves the risk of finding something unexpected in the text, finding out something unexpected about oneself. The risk is not only that the trauma revealed may reverberate in the reader if they allow themselves to identify with the narrator but that, as an effect of this, the reader may come face to face with their own repressed experiences of pain and trauma.

There are fundamental resistances to becoming the type of reader, listener, or witness who is able to make an appropriate and adequate response to narratives and to those who speak them. As Marcia Langton points out, a great many non-Aboriginal representations of Aboriginal people revolve around racist stereotypes which position Aboriginal people as 'other': as objects rather than subjects (Langton 1993:40). Objectivity insists on distance. The 'othering' of Aboriginal people allows non-Aboriginal people to distance themselves from Aboriginal people and thus to refuse engagement.

Iris Marion Young links racism to our fear of the 'otherness' within ourselves. Our sense of identity is threatened by the possibility of 'becoming other' (Young 1990:129). The greater the distance between ourselves and others, the safer we feel. Difference becomes a landscape whose unfamiliarity both frightens and fascinates us. We view it with curiosity while reassuring ourselves and others that it is too difficult to traverse, and thus we protect ourselves from confronting our fears.

Consequently, as is evidenced in contemporary Australian discourse about Aboriginal people, there is a desire to maintain Aboriginal people as safely and recognisably 'other'. While Aboriginal people who experienced removal and other forms of dispossession were long refused recognition by the State, 'traditional Aboriginality' has simultaneously been promoted nationally and internationally in a move to provide Australia with an ancient history and a unique (non-racist) identity (Lattas 1990). The Aboriginal people who are represented become objectified as cultural symbols in a way which, as well as being depoliticising, sustains the perception that 'real' Aboriginal people are both temporally and spatially distant from other Australians and thus outside the possibility of subjective engagement.

Aboriginal people who are excluded by such selective appropriation continue to be regarded as a problem – perhaps even still as a 'half-caste problem', to use the racist terminology of the not so distant past. But it is precisely those Aboriginal people whose lives have been determined by the policies and practices of removal and may indeed 'look white' who constitute a threat to the maintenance of a (mythical) 'mainstream white identity'.

In this way, Aboriginal people who experienced the trauma of removal continue to be overlooked and/or victimised. They are not 'black' enough to be paraded as a source of national pride, they are not 'white' enough to blend silently into the background. They are not 'authentically other', but neither are they safely the same. Their differences are simultaneously asserted and repudiated. They are too demanding. They want recognition ('but they're not really different so why should they receive any 'special' attention'), they want apologies ('but it wasn't "us" who hurt them'), they want compensation ('but don't they already get enough hand outs?'), they insist on 'digging up the past' and by doing so disturb the smooth surface of the present that we wish so much to believe in.

Becoming a witness

Gaynor teaches social anthropology and Jane teaches social policy, both at university level. Nancy often spoke to our classes as a guest lecturer. When she did so, it was not uncommon for the whole group to experience a crisis as a result of their experience of witnessing. Some students reported that after listening to Nancy they found themselves unable to speak, grasping for something appropriate to say but unable to find the words, even in tears. Student evaluation forms frequently noted Nancy's class as the most life changing experience of their semester. One international student told Gaynor how she rushed off after class to ring her mother in the United States to tell her about Nancy's talk – in other words, to find someone who could bear witness to her own trauma of bearing witness. However, as Felman (1992:47ff.) has noted, our attempts to communicate our experiences of witnessing to others often feel inadequate, the words do not seem to speak more than fragments of what we have experienced in the listening. It can be an isolating feeling. We find it hard to connect with others who haven't shared the experience of witnessing.

How much harder it is for the person whose trauma we bear witness to. How many years of isolation and disconnection have they felt before they could begin to speak and ask others to bear witness. And how unbearably painful it is when that other cannot do so, when she or he rejects the demands of bearing witness. Nancy often talked to us about her loneliness. It was a theme of her life. Not having the constancy of family and friends is one thing – but having no one to bear witness to one's pain is a deeper loneliness still. This loneliness also comes from not being able to share our joy, wonder or laughter – things we ought to be able to take for granted in the ups and downs of daily life spent among people who care, who help us to continually become by being our addressable other.

To bear witness is to move towards another person, rather than to expect that person to deny the trauma of their experiences so that we can remain comfortable. Working on this book hasn't always been easy. Not only have we had to negotiate which stories to tell and the ways in which they might best be 'heard', we – Gaynor, Jane and Anna – have needed to listen and re-listen, to be ongoing witnesses to Nancy's pain. Even after many accounts, it is hard to deal with the emotions such listening evokes. How strong Nancy had to become in order to share her story publicly, resolute in her belief that this was the way to ensure it would not happen again.

Gaynor, Jane and Nancy were friends for many years before the writing of this book began – long before Nancy spoke at Parliament House, before her grandchildren were born, before she found her mother. In response to Nancy's desire to publish her story, Jane and Gaynor started taping her when she spoke to student groups, community groups and conferences, and recorded her telling her story during hours spent together at home, at university, picnicking in parks and visiting places of Nancy's childhood.

'Too loud not to hear'

Nancy was an evocative speaker and it was a way of ensuring that she could tell her story in her own way. We discovered that each time she spoke to a group she would bring out different themes, tell of different events. She never 'prepared', and always spoke from her heart about her experiences. This meant that she would often go all over the place as she took her listeners through episodes from her turbulent life.

It was Anna's research on trauma and removal narratives that helped Gaynor and Jane to better understand the role and the implications of being a witness. Her work contributed in significant ways to our ability to reflect on our relationship with Nancy, and on our shared aims in writing this book. As well as incorporating her research into this book, Anna transcribed the tapes and reworked the resulting text into a more fluid narrative form, as well as doing much of the background research to contextualise Nancy's story.

People can't be named – even when they should thanked for reaching out to Nancy, as one human being to another. For Nancy these were rare but precious memories – and we hope some of these people will recognise themselves. Others would not want their treatment of a young Aboriginal child to be made public, even though it should have been. We can only hope that other children did not suffer from these same people's attitudes and actions.

As co-writers, we have been privileged not just to hear and bear witness to Nancy's story but to have shared our lives and stories with Nancy too. Nancy gave us inspiration and strength in incalculable ways. If our book can bring a small part of that into your life, we will have accomplished our task.

My story begins ...
can you possibly comprehend?

A beautiful old house ...
There's a beautiful old house in Glebe called Bidura. That was the Children's Home in my younger days. It was called the 'Depot' – isn't that terrible, to call it a depot where they take the kids back and then farm them out again?

It was both black and white children there. I can remember being upstairs in that top room and looking out the window and seeing in the garden all the white kids with visitors. And we used to think, why have they got visitors and we haven't? Our people were not allowed to come near us. We were told that they didn't want us.

I was under how many systems? Child Welfare, Church Missionary Society, Aboriginal Welfare Board. They all had a go! Trying to reform me, trying to make me in the mould of being a good little white girl, and all those foster families....

First, my mother and I were staying at a place called Correlli, in Livingstone Road, Marrickville, opposite the Catholic Church. It was a home for mothers and young babies. She tried to keep me. She kept me for 15 months. She tried ... they took me away – because I was fair.

She stayed in Harris Street, Ultimo. There used to be a Salvation Army Hostel at Stanmore. She stayed there. I would go past there and look at it and think, 'You walked here.'

From one home to another ...
First, I was with a family, the A family at Merrylands. They were Seventh Day Adventists. They were very good to me, very kind, and I thought I belonged to them. They were gentle people, very, very gentle people, and I was given a good home and treated very well. I used to call her Mum and him Dad, and there was a little white boy who I called my brother. We used to fight. I remember fighting with him and once I bit him. My foster mother came out then and bit my hand!

Nancy in her bus (2003). Photographer unknown.

I cried! And I did not bite him again.

My life was pretty happy there. I felt safe. I felt secure. My earliest memory is waking up in a grey cot and there was a doll at the end of the bed, and it had brown eyes. It was Christmas time.

My mother went out there to my foster mother at Merrylands. She found out I was there and she came out to see me. I didn't find this out until my first son was born 23 years later, when I took him to meet this foster mother. They were a wonderful family and I loved them dearly – even if they had some warped ideas at times. They were kind-hearted people.

I took Peter back for them to meet this baby of mine and she said to me, 'Never have anything to do with the Aboriginal Welfare Board. Never have anything to do with Child Welfare.' And I said, 'Why?' And she told me that when my mother came out to visit me she had been told that I would be able to go with her if she got a job, a live-in job as a maid. So she did come back, all excited because she had found a job at Ivanhoe. But, lo and behold, I wasn't allowed to go with her, and she wasn't allowed to come out and visit any more. It wasn't long after that they eventually must have decided that it was a bit dangerous leaving me there so they moved me on. Ruby never saw me again. She never saw me again.

One day my foster Dad put me in the front seat of the Model-T Ford. The family were all standing there with their hankies, 'Bye, bye'. I'm thinking, why are they crying? I turned round to look at them – and there on the back seat were all my things, all my dolls. I became really frightened then. I started to cry because I couldn't understand why they were saying goodbye to me. I couldn't understand it at all. When I think back, I was almost unable to think, I was so frightened, this was the first move.

They were moving me on from there. My file said it was because I was sexually promiscuous. I was five! You know why I was sexually promiscuous? Ross, the little white boy that was living there with them, and me, they used to bath us together. I can remember to this day, so clear, that when they got him down in the water, he used to scream when they'd be washing the soap off his hair. And here's this little thing sitting up there and I said, 'Oh, what's that?' I remember getting a hiding for that. Not long after that I was moved. That's all I can think, that they'd have said they couldn't cope with me because I was sexually promiscuous!

I was taken to another family down in Marrickville. To go from a Seventh Day Adventist home, where there was no alcohol, to a home where she dyed her hair bright red with henna, and they were always drunk and always fighting, it was very frightening. It was the most terrible part of my life. I didn't last there very long. I slept on a black ottoman under the stairs. It was one of those curly ottomans with the backs on it. My bed. And they used to twist my arm up against my back when they got drunk. I must have been very sick when I was there and they were writing very accusing letters about the A family. Mrs A had taken me to see Dr Brown at Parramatta, but this one wrote letters saying I was sick and the other family had done nothing about it. But that was wrong because the A family was very good to me, they really were.

After about six weeks she must have decided I wasn't what she was looking for to lavish all her love on. She must have told the Child Welfare that she didn't want me and must have instructed them to take me to Bidura.

Bidura

Bidura is another story altogether. The matron was an obese brute. She had glasses which enlarged her eyes, and she was a terrifying woman. It was there I found out I was Aboriginal. I was in Bidura when the King died, old King George V died. They had this mournful music coming through in the dining room on these speakers and we were told, 'All stand up!' We were having bread with honey on it, the honey had gone hard, and hot cocoa. It was one of my favourite meals, I thought it was wonderful, chomping into it. So when I heard 'Stand up, everybody, stand up!' I thought, I'm not standing up, I'm going to sit here and have my bread and my hot cocoa. Because that's what I thought was more important when I was five. Who wouldn't?

'Oh you naughty girl, you naughty girl, get in the corner, get in the corner.' I knew very well about the corner, being stood in the corner became a constant in my life. So there I was standing in the corner and I just happened to turn around and here was an Aboriginal girl with an afro hairdo. Her hair had been allowed to grow long and it had gone sort of afro, and she was a lot darker than me. I screamed, I got an awful fright. I don't think I'd seen another Aboriginal person before that. The nurse, Nurse McGrath, I'll never forget her name, came over and grabbed hold of me and shook me and she said, 'You stupid little girl, you're just like her.' And I'm thinking, now wait a minute, you know, I can't be.

That's how I found out I was Aboriginal. Once I found out I was different, I began to notice, or maybe it fell into place, that there were different things happening in my life. After I found out I was Aboriginal, I started to become quite cynical for a child. Quite rebellious. I was beginning to hate everybody.

We used to have to step up into the bath, to save the staff in the home from bending down and having to bathe 50 kids. The bath was high and it was easier to stand up and get the kid to walk up and get into the bath. We'd march up to the bath and get in and they'd scrub us and we'd get out. I remember marching up the steps and looking out and here was the gardener standing there watching us, you know. One of the things we'd been taught in this home was girls should be modest. I can remember in my childlike way thinking, girls should be modest, and they're allowing this to happen. So there's a whole set of rules for us and a whole set of rules for the rest of society. I was finding this out in a very quick way. Very quickly.

People would take me into their home for the novelty of having a little Aboriginal child. 'Look how good I am.' Their intentions were probably well meant, but as soon as the novelty wore off and the little Aboriginal child became a normal child who did naughty things, she would be sent back. Rejected once again. Rejection is something I put up with all my life. I used to cry. Dear God, I used to cry! And it was from sheer loneliness.

A foster home in Arncliffe

After that, I went to a family in Arncliffe. I don't know whether she had a husband or not, I never saw him, but she had a bloody big Alsatian dog. It must have been around Christmas time I went there 'cos I can remember us all being taken out to look up and see Santa Claus in an aeroplane! She lived in a house which backed onto the Princes Highway at Arncliffe there. I think there's a lot of flats built there now. I'd come out and go across an overhead bridge to go to the school up on the top of the rock ledge. There were a lot of rocks and the school was on top of them.

There was this little blonde sheila with curly hair – if I met her now she'd be gone! She was a spiteful little thing. We had those chalk boxes then and they had our pencils in, real sharp. She'd come up to my desk and get a pencil, break it and then hand it to me. Then I'd get in trouble for breaking my pencil. It was a power thing with her, I guess. I think this inbred superiority of the whiteman was being handed down to these kids and these are the ones you can hear now that are fully denying that it ever happened in their day.

Then back to Bidura ...

When we were at Bidura, people would come to interview the matron and pick out a child. You had to walk up this verandah towards the matron sitting there with her glasses, terrifying you in case you made a wrong move. You had to stand there with the usual hands behind your back, head down. You were introduced, you had to shake hands with the lady and say, 'How do you do? I'm very pleased to meet you.' Then they'd discuss you in front of you, then you'd go back down full of suspense whether you were going to leave this dreadful place and be taken away by these wonderful people who were going to give you a home and look after you, or whether you were going to be lining up for tea again that night.

Chatswood

When Mrs M from Chatswood came and decided to have me, I went there, and had a reasonably happy life. You've got to remember good times, haven't you. We lived near a bakery and I used to go up and the bakers used to give us a little bit of dough and I had a paint tin I would put it in. It would be hot weather, see – this is a children thing – and I used to stick the dough into this hot tin and leave it out in the sun and hope it would bake. Just the normal things that children do.

I went to Willoughby Primary School and I still remember the teachers. I had a teacher called Miss B. She hated me, even though my foster parents had a good home. I was in the choir and I loved singing. We had to have dresses made from paisley patterned material and a scarf made from paisley material. But you know what colour they got for me? White. Again I was being made to feel different, separate. I so much wanted a paisley patterned dress. That white one was probably the best quality material and the best quality everything but it wasn't what was required and I felt so unhappy, so different.

My story begins ...

I had a boyfriend called Kenny B. I've always remembered his name because I saw The Mikado, the movie, with Kenny B at the old Chatswood cinema. They used to send me to the movies every Saturday afternoon. Edith Cavell and The Mikado was the big thing. The Drum was the first technicolour movie. It was really very exciting, the colours. These movies, the dramas, all these old, old movies that I still see now and again, this is where I first saw them, at this theatre at Chatswood. We'd walk from home. We used to walk and Kenny used to come and pick me up to go at about six or seven, and he'd always walk on the right side of me, so he was always next to the gutter. In those days that was the done thing. I used to say, Don't! Don't! I can remember saying that but he'd want to walk on the right side. Kenny B – I'll never forget his name. Isn't that funny, what you remember. We'd have pigs trotter soup every Saturday night. I hated it. I've never had pig trotters soup since.

And we'd go past this house and in the shed of the house they had this old working model of a biscuit making machine, for an Arnott's biscuit! I can remember that very, very clearly and we'd always run in there and have a look. I mean, we'd see it every weekend, but we still had to go in there and have a look!

I lost an orange balloon down there, at that family's home. I'd been given an orange balloon, I don't know where from. It might have been a birthday or something. I was out there playing with it. There was this fence, and then there was this drop, and down there was a highway. I'd say that was Roseville Chase. And you'd look down onto that. We were sort of up on this hill where it was all bush. The wind took this balloon and I watched it go for miles and miles. You could just see this orange balloon for miles and miles, until I couldn't see it any longer ...

On the way to school there was a persimmon tree. You never seem to get persimmons now, not growing in a yard. They used to hang over the fence and I never used to pinch them because it was just a little bit too high for me, just a little bit. Somehow I could never reach it. The old lady who lived in there came out one day and she said, 'I've watched you and you've never stolen a persimmon, so here's a boxful.' And no, I didn't steal them either! Because I wasn't tall enough.

Funny, eh! They were just so delicious. The skin would make your mouth feel a bit funny and you'd have to eat them with a spoon. 'I've noticed you didn't steal any. Here's a boxful.' And I got this boxful of persimmons!

Another time pump up scooters were in. They must have been the first ones that ever came out with real pump tyres. At the top of the hill, you could come down, and turn that way to Willoughby. On the top of that hill this little girl said, 'Oh Nancy, do you want a go of my scooter?' And I thought, 'Yeah, wow!' And off I went and fell off at the bottom. The road had just been top levelled, you know when they just top level and they haven't rolled it yet with the roller. I took the skin off my arms, and she came down and she got such a fright that she just grabbed the scooter and ran for her life and never stopped to see how I was. I was sitting there bawling my eyes out and some women came out and they got me home and I got all fixed up.

Going to school we used to have to run around in circles on the floor – remember the old circles they used to paint on the floor? We used to have to run around those with our arms bent up to touch our shoulders, but because my arms were bandaged I couldn't put my hands on my shoulders. I remember Miss B, the teacher, smacking me. I can remember it very clearly. She had short black hair, and she hit me because I couldn't put my arms up. 'You're lazy, you're lazy!' she said. Another time a group of us that used to go to school, we pinched these peaches and they were green. We got sick. I remember that very clearly too.

I did get sexually assaulted at two different families. I was seven when the first assault happened and eleven when the second one happened. And when I think about it, when I think about it, God Almighty!

I had been sent to buy eggs from the shop and I had my school bag on my back. In those days they used to put half a dozen eggs in a paper bag and twist it round. I was running home with them when a friend of the family stopped me. It wasn't someone in the family, it was a friend of their son who raped me in the bushland gully near my home. I knew who he was, he went to an exclusive private school. I remember him telling me, 'This is what happens when you get married.'

When he ran away, I jumped up and ran screaming, screaming home. What also frightened me was where the eggs had broken in the bag on my back, and they were running down the back of my dress and onto my legs and I didn't know what it was. It was the most terrifying thing because I could feel it, this gunk running down my legs and I didn't know what it was. I ran into the house and the kitchen was that dreadful bright cream and green they used to have in those days. I told that foster mother what had happened. They didn't put their arms around me to comfort me. She just went over to the drawer and got a knife out. 'Don't you tell anybody or we'll cut your tongue out. Don't you ever let me hear you talk like that again.' Well, of course, a child that age, seven and a half years, you believe them. I couldn't walk for two days, not properly, but that family, they couldn't have cared less. They just kept me home from school.

What damage he did to me, I don't know, but they were able to pick it up when I went back to Bidura later on, because the doctor who checked you out, he knew straight away something had gone on. 'Oh, you've been letting spiders crawl up you!' he said to me. That was a long time after, but it made me so angry. I couldn't say anything. Long after, he could probably still see some of the damage that had been done.

I just hated going back to Bidura. Every time you went back there, from when you were tiny, you were made to put on one of the nighties. Oh, I hate thinking about it. And this dreadful old doctor used to do an internal examination on every child while matron was standing there. They made me feel like a criminal when they examined me after what had happened to me. They just made me feel so terrible.

The 'whipping boy'

Then I went to a family at Bankstown. They had everything. They had a nice little home. It wasn't a big home, they had a car, they had everything they needed. I went to Brownies, I learned tennis and swimming at Bankstown Pool when it was open. We went to Bankstown School.

I liked it when the family had a car because you usually got to go out. He had quite a good job, and we used to go to the beach. I can remember being down at one of the beaches, it might have been Cronulla, where they used to have donkey rides or whatever, and I must have done something wrong. She was hitting me, belting me near the car. But what was hurting more was that I still had sand on me and that was making it sting more. I remember that very clearly.

But everything that went wrong in that house, I was the whipping boy. I woke up one night and I could hear them talking and I could hear their daughter crying. She was 12 and I was 8, and I could hear my name being mentioned all the time. The next minute this woman came in and she started to belt the shit out of me. And I'm thinking, why? Why is she always belting me? She woke me up in the night and blamed me for teaching her daughter how to lie. Here she was bashing me in the middle of the night – well, it seemed like the middle of the night but it couldn't have been that late – and telling me that it was all my fault that her daughter lied. What had happened, her daughter hadn't brought home her school report because it wasn't what she thought Mummy was expecting. And so it was my fault. I'd taught their daughter to lie. So I was just a scapegoat for anything that went on in the family. They were terribly negative. I suppose I was lucky that I was strong enough to stand up and take it. A lot of our poor people weren't able to.

They were just a normal working people. He had a job with Sunshine, you know, that made all the cans of milk. Some sort of executive job with them. He used to go off in a suit and when he came home we always used to go out to different places like the beach or something like that. On Friday night we'd go out, because Friday night was late night shopping then. Sometimes we'd go to the pictures. I remember going to see 'The Cat and The Canary' but they got up and walked out. I remember thinking, Why? Why? This is a bloody good picture! – spooky, you know! They wouldn't let us watch it, you see. It wasn't good for children.

But I wasn't happy there at all and they took me back to Bidura.

I was getting to know Aboriginal girls at Bidura. We were getting to know each other. There were times that I was happy. Like when I was sent back to Bidura and I'd see other Koori girls and I'd think, Oh great, here we go, what can we do now? When we came back to

My story begins ...

Bidura, we'd automatically seek each other out. Gloria and Violet, they were two of my best friends. It was funny, the Koori kids were the ones who just laughed and got through it. Our weird sense of humour kept us going I guess.

We'd get up to some terrible things, like the time we were going to run away. We thought that if we could run up the coke heap and jump over that fence, we'd be right. It had been raining and I can remember saying to Gloria, 'You go first.' And she said, 'No you go first.' This went on for about 20 minutes and anyway next thing I got up the gumption and up I went, up the coke. It was so wet and slippery, that I just went slooosh – and slid down! So Gloria's rolling around on the grass laughing. I called her 'F N B' – because we hadn't learn how to swear then!

I got up and I had another go, by this time she was helpless with laughing. I didn't think I was ever going to make it up. So next time I said to myself, 'Well I'm not going to let this coke heap win.' So I ran and I jumped and got to the top of the fence. I dragged myself up and finally I got up there. Then it was her turn, and when we'd both jumped over the fence we were almost too weak to run. Our socks were black from the coke, but we thought we looked normal, so off down the lane we went, right down the back there at Pyrmont, right down the back there at Glebe, at Harold Park and right down along the water. We got picked up not long after that – and we wondered why.

Another time we were going to shoot through, four of us, after tea, we were going to shoot through. We were Edna and Wilma – two blondes – then me and Esther, two blacks. We had curly hair, both of us. So we were going to shoot through, 'Right Oh, you!' Off we were going to go. So we get to the gate. But then I got chicken! Edna's going, here, 'Have my ring, have my ring,' she's got this ring on that was made out of a piece of aircraft, during the war, see. She gives me this ring, so I went too.

We got right down to Broadway near the Uni there, the four of us. Then the police came along. I don't know why they wanted to pick on us. How'd they found out? But we were only kids. We would have only been about nine or ten. They had a square car with a gas thing on the back, the old gas boxes, remember, instead of the petrol. Anyway, they took us for a ride! Right over the Harbour Bridge. Bought us ice-cream, took us down to the Central Police Station, kept us there, fed us lollies, and when we started getting too tired they said, 'Come on kids, we better take you back!' It was great. So we were ready to go again the next day.

In the meantime, there was this bloody old bitch, Matron P. Any girls or boys – we did have little boys there, too – who were inmates of Bidura can tell you about Matron P, and I bet they've all got the same thing to say about her. She was a very big woman, big boobs. She used to wear a veil – what on earth for, I don't know, I don't think she was a registered nurse – and glasses that magnified her eyes. So she was a pretty terrifying apparition to come up against when you were young.

We come dragging through the gate and there she was standing, with her hands folded and I thought, 'Oh shit!' She took us inside, downstairs to the bathroom, we all had to get into the bath and she was belting us with the bath brush as she's washing us, scrubbing us with it. She gave us a dose of castor oil each, put a nightie on us and made us stand for punishment, for I don't know how long. We were nearly dropping off to sleep.

But I was beginning to feel different. I noticed that I was beginning to be treated in a different way to the other children. I noticed that I was being excluded from things. It was quite obvious and I was getting a feeling that I wasn't as good as the other kids. I can remember feeling very angry and this was beginning to show in my behaviour, because, boy, was I a rebel. I just refused to comply and was always in trouble. And of course every time I was in trouble I was being told it was because I was Aboriginal, bad, lazy. The usual stereotyping was very obvious in those days because I think they firmly believed all those things.

If somebody were to write a book just on what happened at Bidura ... I can remember being awake one night hearing all these kids crying, screaming and crying and crying. The next day when, we woke up there were some new kids there. It was these new kids being brought in, 'Mummy! Mummy! Mummy!' they were shouting. Those sorts of things do touch you when you are a child. That's probably why I'm such a softie with our kids now, because I couldn't bear to think of them like that. It would break my heart if they were going to take them and put them in a home like that and split them up.

Moved – again ...
The Strathfield family I went to were a different sort of family altogether. She had a green dress with white daisies on it, a crepe de chine dress. I can remember her very clearly, very clearly. This little brown straw hat and brown suede shoes. I remember the day she took me back to Strathfield. I remember us getting off the bus, and her daughter running down the road yelling, 'Whoopee, whoopee, here comes my new sister.'

We got up to the house and there was their baby. I fell in love with that child from that minute. Here was a little boy who didn't give a damn whether I was Aboriginal or not, who grew up loving me as a sister. When he was about ten or eleven he was being told that I wasn't his real sister and he was saying, 'Well, I'll marry her when I grow up and then she'll be part of this family'. He and I never had an argument. I love him dearly and whenever I see him he and his wife accept me as just Nancy, whether I'm Koori or not. I loved my foster brother very much. He's still alive and I would no more hurt him than a fly because he was a gentle, beautiful person. He was then and he still is. But he doesn't understand Aboriginal problems, no. Because he was brought up in that era. I suppose he was 6 years younger than me so he probably didn't comprehend the problems that I was having to deal with. Like being told I was dirty all the time – all the time. He's a retired bank manager now. He wouldn't have known what was going on in those days. He wouldn't have known. He wouldn't have known what my unhappiness was and he couldn't have understood. He probably wouldn't have been aware of all the horrible things his Mum was doing to me. I think she was secretive about some of the things she did. He was a real innocent child who probably wouldn't think badly of anybody. I know he was hurt badly too. Later, he went to work in Port Hedland, and she used to sit out looking at the stars and thinking, 'I'm looking at the stars and so is he'. Of course he wasn't. She went down to Head Office and got him shifted back. He was furious, absolutely furious. That's what she was like. She was so possessive.

He loved the trains. His Dad was on the railways and would take him up to meet all the drivers who were working on Strathfield Station. They'd lift him onto the trains. His Dad wasn't a train driver himself but forty years he'd worked on Ashfield Station, God love him. So he wanted to be a train driver. Right or wrong, he wanted to be a train driver! But his mother, oh no, she couldn't have her little boy dirtying his hands on the trains. 'Oh, look at their dirty hands!' I can remember her saying it. 'No, no, don't do that, he'll get dirty.'

She was very religious. She was a Christian. And in those days being Christian meant that you were very narrow minded. She was very uncompromising in everything, she was not very flexible at all. She led me merry hell. She'd reject me one minute and send me away, and then love me the next minute and want me back.

She used to take me out to Yarra Bay Beach, down past La Perouse Mission. In those days they weren't the houses that are there now, there were old green and yellow houses and they were not in very good repair. She'd say to me, 'Look at them, look at them, they're all dirty. Look! Look! They're all drunk.' And I'd be looking at them and thinking, well, they don't look too bad to me. I wanted to run over and say to them, 'Do you know Ruby?', which I knew was my mother's name. But she was trying to brainwash me and make me think that my people were no good.

I wouldn't wear red for years because she told me, Aboriginals all wear red. I wouldn't wear red for years because I thought it was wrong or there was something horrible about wearing red. Now I know she didn't want me to wear it because it was a 'power' colour. But in those days, you know, you were brainwashed into thinking these things. I used to feel so patriotic when they played Rule Britannia. Oh wow! Because I was being brought up in this type of society. And God Save the King or the Queen, it was the King in those days, and you'd stand up.

We had a neat cat – Fluffy was its name. It was a beautiful animal and I loved it dearly. He was an inside cat. He wouldn't go and pee in the corner, he peed down the hole in the bathroom. We've got a cat

My story begins ...

La Perouse

La Perouse was named after the French navigator and explorer La Perouse, who landed there in January 1788. An Aboriginal presence at La Perouse was recorded in an 1812 sketch made during a French expedition of an Aboriginal man called Timbere, probably a relative of the Timbery family who still live in the area. From about 1880, there has been a permanent settlement of Aborigines at La Perouse living on land said to have been unofficially granted to Queen Emma Timbery. Many of these people were originally from the south coast. In 1883, the Aboriginal camp was established as a reserve under the Aborigines Protection Board and houses were erected. Initially the camp was controlled by missionaries and police, then later managers were installed.

In the late 1920s the Aboriginal settlement was moved back from where it had been because the houses were sinking in the sand. During the depression of the 1920s-1930s, there were a lot of unemployed living at La Perouse in makeshift houses. The two camps north of the reserve were known as Happy Valley and Hill 60, which were mostly inhabited by whites. South of the reserve was the predominantly Aboriginal camp, Frog Hollow. In the early 1950s the camps were broken up by the local council. The white people moved away and the Aboriginal people moved onto the reserve, into Tasman Street or out of the area.

In 1973 when the Board was abolished, control of the homes on the reserve was taken over by the Housing Commission in conjunction with the Aboriginal Lands Trust. In 1983 Local Land Councils were established giving the Aboriginal inhabitants control over their own land and homes, including Yarra Bay House.

Source: Individual Heritage Group 1987.

now who will go and do exactly the same thing. Whether it's the smell that attracts them or what I'm not sure.

I remember getting woken up, it was dark and I'd been asleep. I was being hit with a piece of dressed wood. It would have been about two by one inch, and she was hitting me with that – that foster mother– and calling me a dirty little black gin for weeing down the hole. Anyway a few days later, she caught the cat – she actually saw it – and you know what, she never said sorry to me. That passed through my mind, even though I was only a little girl, 'Why couldn't she say sorry?'

I remember once, during the war, at Strathfield Park there was a searchlight display put on by the army. All the people were going up there to see it. That day, I'd eaten my lunch and didn't eat my crusts. So I wrapped them up and left them in my case. She spread castor oil on those crusts and made me sit there, in the park and eat them. The whole time she was pinching either my arm or my ear. I hated this lady. Sometimes I hated her so much. And yet at other times she could be so gentle with me. Being a soft kind of person even as a child, I would think, 'She loves me, she really loves me and things are going to be different from now on.' And then she'd turn around, and do something to me that was horrible. These mental cruelties were awful. And the physical cruelties. She was forever beating me.

I would become so desperately unhappy there at times. In the medicine cupboard recessed into the wall, they had some stuff with a brush that they used to paint your throat with. On it was written 'Poison,' which probably meant that you had to treat it with care – so I drank some. When I look back I think to myself, why would a child do that? A child can feel that desperately unhappy. I wanted to die. But it was just this vile taste and nothing happened. And I remember thinking to myself, 'Oh well, so much for that.'

They didn't have a car, because they didn't believe in driving. We didn't ride on a bus on Sunday, whether it was stinking hot or not, we had to walk from Strathfield up to St Thomas's in Enfield every day. In the morning, up and back again to Sunday School, up and back again in the night. You didn't drive a car on Sundays, you see. The funny thing was that poor old Dad used to work on the railways on Sunday but I never used to hear them kicking up a fuss about that. He was a nice old fellow, he just used to sail along. But she was erratic. She had a spontaneous abortion and blamed me! So that didn't sit happily with me.

I kept in touch with that foster Dad, though. He loved my daughter, Megan, just loved her! He was retired, and he used to take Megan on a Saturday so I could go dancing down near Burwood Park. Everyone called him the general, because they loved him, and he used to get everyone organised, you see. I don't know if I ever heard him raise his voice. He was that sort of person. He was a gentle, accepting, henpecked man. How on earth he didn't punch the shit out of her, I don't know. And he worked hard all those years and everything.

I heard that she and her daughter were terrible to him towards the end. Megan used to get upset. When he died they didn't even let Megan know. Megan rang and wanted to know why and they started to run me down. 'Look,' she said to them, 'don't you run my mother down. My mother's done a lot for me. My mother's worked very hard to do what she did, now you leave her alone.' But they kept it up and kept it up. Megan slammed the phone down and never spoke to them again.

My foster brother said to me last time I saw him, 'Where is she, is she still alive?' That was his own sister he was talking about. So that would give you some sort of idea of the warped situation we were all living under. I was not happy there, and yet even later on she'd keep on wanting to take me back. She was the one that kept coming back for me. She wanted to be seen to be doing the right Christian thing, the good thing. She was the one who said, 'Oh Nancy has been very good, she's even washed her neck.' Once she said, 'We feel Nancy would be happier with the dark people.' And I said, 'Yes, bloody oath, she would be!'

That's what happened once the novelty wore off, you know, 'Look at these good people with the little Aboriginal child.' Once that wore off and the naughtiness started to come out, they thought I was too much trouble.

That day I was talking in Parliament, I came out later and drove past the old Births, Deaths and Marriages Registry. I remembered taking myself in there when I was ten and I thought, Gee, I never thought that I would be talking in Parliament when I went into that building there looking for my mother. The old man in there then – he seemed old to me, he was probably in his 20s, you know! – he got the big book out, blew all the dust off it, and opened it to show me where she'd signed to register me. But in the meantime he'd rung the police that I was there. I must have known her name. I'm not too sure where I found out her name properly, I can't remember that. I must have known to be able to go in there and ask about her.

Mulgoa

They sent me back to Mulgoa Mission. They thought a Church mission was the type of home to put me in. They stuck me out there because at Mulgoa there were Aboriginal people that had been brought down from the Northern Territory. They were sent down there because of the war. I remember them 'cos I had a crush on one of the boys, Jack. He was a nice boy and I often wonder what happened to him, whether he went back up there or what. They were all removed. Some of the mothers came with their kids. We used to walk to the old Mulgoa Church and then we used to go to Mulgoa School, but I didn't last very long there.

Another family in Eastwood ...

After I left Mulgoa they sent me to this family where the man was a Reverend, a Minister. They had a daughter called Nancy so I couldn't be called Nancy. "What do you want to be called?" I said, "Anything will do." So they gave me a book with Aboriginal names in it, and I picked Kruby, which meant Waratah. I picked Kruby only because it was like Ruby, see.

Well, all I seemed to do was clean the house and feed the baby. When I had time to do my own thing, they had this big garden, sort of a bit of an orchard on the side of the rectory, it was a beautiful old home, one of those lovely old federation homes, and I used to go out there and dance with the trees. I had a real good imagination, thank God.

It must have been when I was just starting to go to high school when they sent me up to Hornsby Domestic Science School. Then they found out that I had things in my hair. I must have got them when I was up at the Mission but they cut all my hair off. I wouldn't go to school without any hair so I used to wear a hat all the time.

But the Reverend interfered with me. I used to try and get away from him. I tried to get away. He didn't actually rape me, it was all ... horrible stuff. And the Bishop, I always remember him. He came to dinner one night and I was introduced to him. He was a dear old man, very kind, and I wanted to tell him. But I think this fella knew I was going to, and they whisked me away before I could say anything. So

My story begins ...

Mulgoa

Mulgoa is located 60 km west of Sydney at the foot of the Blue Mountains. In the 1940s when Nancy was there (1944) it was still a rural area. In 1942, the Commonwealth Government evacuated a number of 'half-caste' Aboriginal children from Northern Territory (many from Groote Eylandt) as a precaution in the event of any invasion during World War II. They were sent to Mulgoa and placed in the care of the Church Missionary Society in an old Rectory. Many of their parents followed and found employment as domestics in the town.

The Rectory building had two storeys and a cellar. In his autobiography, *Saltwater fella*, John Moriarty (2000) recalls that the five youngest boys, himself included, slept in the cellar. The Anglican missionaries who ran the home gave the children English names and would only allow them to speak English – they were forbidden to speak their tribal languages. However, the elders continued to do so in secret and in this way managed to share their language, stories and culture with the children, tell them who they were, who their families were, and give them a sense of pride in their Aboriginality.

Younger children attended the local school and mixed well with the local community and older children worked as domestics and cooks. Moriarty recalls that they were always hungry at the mission and often searched for bush tucker and went hunting to supplement the meagre mission food. He was once asked if he wanted to be adopted but, like some of the other boys, he declined, preferring to remain with his friends.

In 1945, 27 of the children were returned to the Northern Territory leaving 21 at Mulgoa. In 1948, the Mission was closed and the remaining children sent away, the girls to St Mary's Hospital, Alice Springs, and the boys to St Francis Hostel in Semaphore, Adelaide.

Source: Moriarty 2000:22–65; various newspapers of 1949.

that was that. I ran away from him one time and I ran into this other house and told them and said 'I'm never going to go back there,' and it wasn't long after that I was moved away.

But in my papers it said that Nancy is running around telling lies about the Reverend, so I think I wasn't believed. The first place I got assaulted I was told they were going to cut my tongue out but at this place they didn't bother. I was just telling lies. 'You're only a little liar, little black liar', that's what was said to me. 'Aboriginal people tell terrible lies. Aboriginal people always drink, they're always drunk.'

The Reception Centre

They put me into the Reception Centre. They were saying I was mad. I remember I was there for three weeks, being assessed I suppose, but the food was wonderful. You just sat around in bed all day, I loved it. And of course being so young, the nurses just thoroughly spoiled me. It was like a big holiday. It was a new thing for me being spoiled. But they decided I wasn't crazy, so I was sent back to the Strathfield family. That didn't last long.

Cootamundra

Next they sent me down to the Aboriginal Girls' Home at Cootamundra. I was uncontrollable and they thought this would be the place to really straighten me out. Needless to say, it didn't.

I can remember running away from there and drinking bore water, because it was so bloody hot out on the road. I thought I'd poisoned myself, and was that glad when the police came along in their car and caught me and took me back. I was very sick when I got there, and nobody believed I was sick until I collapsed one day. As I was getting better, I found this big bottle of aspirin – and I'm lucky to be here today, because I took half of that bottle.

I don't think they could cope with me. I wasn't happy there – the only good thing about the place was the custard they served at mealtimes. Mind you, at that stage, wherever they'd placed me probably wouldn't have worked.

I'm not saying we were unhappy all the time, we weren't. We had a capacity to laugh. A great capacity to laugh. And I loved to read. Thank God I loved to read! And when I was in Cootamundra Girls' Home I had enough books to read. We used to get little paper books or if I'd see a book I'd get it, or a magazine, anything. I had a hiding place up on the roof. I had blankets, pillows and all up there. I used to get up there and lie and read my books. I'd hear them call out to me and I'd just pretend I didn't even hear, go on reading my books. I remember reading *Jane Eyre* and I was only quite young. Our kids find it hard to read the word cat when they're in third class and I don't know why, because reading was so simple to me. There was a brown reader, a red reader, a blue reader. You started from the blue I think and then you went to the red and then the brown or something like that. I can remember those. I loved the smell of them. When I look back on it now I can remember knowing those words so I don't know when I started reading. Maybe I found out, in my childlike way, that it was an escape.

Moonacullah

I was sent down from Cootamundra to Moonacullah. It was like they say in the army, 'We'll send you down!' Well I was being sent down alright. I remember the escort lady. She bought us a sandwich at Junee, I remember eating those sandwiches on the train. I loved train travel. Just loved it. So it wasn't a hard thing for me to put up with.

But I remember driving along and thinking, where am I going to this time? We got further and further away from Sydney, which was my base, where I knew. I wonder where they're sending me this time? I got into this truck at Deniliquin, sitting on the back of this truck with a whole lot of other Blacks. I'd hardly had anything to do with Aboriginal people except the girls in the home. There were men there. I felt so strange. It's 28 miles out of Deniliquin, and we were driving along, we came to the entrance and we were driving up this big long track, and in the distance I could see these little huts. They were built on a square, the manager's little house was here, and a little church was there, and in the middle was a garden patch where they used to have to grow vegetables.

Well, Aboriginal people are not farmers. I can remember them always getting into trouble because they weren't digging up the garden or weeding it or whatever or watering it or something. Probably letting it die.

I went and stayed at the Briggs's house at first. They had houses that were dirt floor and split wood logs. Inside they'd pasted newspaper, then they put this sort of hessian with white paint on it.

And the floors were like polished cement, and they used to throw tea leaves on them to stop the dust going up into everything when they'd sweep out. Tea leaves from the old cup of tea. We used to line up for rations, I can remember doing that very clearly. There were two rooms, one was a sleeping room and one had the stove in it. We never ate inside. We used to eat outside. It was very rare really that you ever cooked anything inside. They always cooked in the big camp ovens, make a fire outside, catch the fish, Murray cod, clean it off, throw it into the pan, and the hot pan would be waiting there, camp oven, cup of billy tea, some johnny cake. You couldn't want for anything more.

There was a school there. They'd ring the bell for school and we'd all go the other way. I suppose that could have been the reason that they thought I was a bad influence on the kids. We thought it was much more fun to raid the orchard or go hunting. This woman had a big quince tree and she lived a bit further on and we used to go down and raid this quince tree.

Old Denny Myers would take us out across the old billabong, I remember it being cracked because of not much rain. Very dry, very cracked and you'd be walking along, crunch, crunch. And he'd be saying, 'Shhhh shhhh'. And we'd all stop and he'd say, 'I can hear.... What was that?' He'd point out that we could hear birds, trees rustling. He'd make us appreciate what was happening around us in the bush. He also taught us how to recognise signs on the ground. Or if there were any little twigs snapped. He taught us the most likely place to find goannas, small things. Mind you I never caught one.

The men in those days still used to go hunting, come back with big kangaroos over their shoulders, and big emu. And when they'd go and come back with a big catch like that, wow! They'd have a big fire, and they used to cook them up on the fire and everybody would be handed their pieces, on a johnny cake. And there was protocol about who had to wait and whose turn it was. And then we'd sit around by the fire and the old people would tell us stories and things like that. And you'd be so frightened you'd sit with your back to the fire, so you could see what was coming up. But I had never had this in my life. So it was pretty amazing. A really amazing feeling. I felt very comfortable with it. I suppose I felt that this was where I belonged.

My story begins ...

There were the Briggs and there were the Days and the Galways and the Ingrams. I wasn't there that long, but I can remember all these family names. Mr Keneer was the manager when I was there and Mary Galway was my best friend. We used to get up to terrible mischief. I suppose it wasn't really terrible when you think about it, because it was just childhood excitement. We hardly ever went into town, but sometimes you were allowed to go into town with the adults when they went to do their shopping or they had to go and see a doctor or something. And you'd run around the town and have a look at it and then you'd be lying down in this park waiting for the truck to come and pick you up. You'd be that bored, waiting to go back out to the old mission.

It was a magic place. If you've ever read Margaret Tucker's book, *If everyone cared*, she's a Moonacullah person, and they took her away from Moonacullah. She says her Mum was working over at Old Morago when they came and got her. Old Morago was the orchard that we used to raid. So how crazy were they? They took her away from a wonderful mother who worked and kept herself immaculate. But they threw me into the place, miles away from anybody I ever knew. How dare they! Then Herron's got the hide to say it didn't happen.

It's in the records that I was a bad influence, that I was cheeky, that I was saying terrible things about the kids. That's not true. I would no more have said anything about the kids because I was happy there. I was happy. And when they sent me away I didn't even have a pair of shoes. They didn't even send me back to Sydney with shoes. I had stone bruises on my feet. Lice in my hair. So they can't go on. They can't go on.

Those photos that were in the paper a few weeks ago, they had this big photo of this yellowy cloud coming up over Griffith. Mate you should have seen the dust storms down there. Nothing on that bit of dust. They were black. They were like those clouds over there. And it'd be rolling and rolling and everybody'd be running around, 'cos as it got nearer the wind got stronger. And everybody would be running around and trying to seal the doors off. When it got to us, it was like turning day into night.

The river there was another amazing, beautiful area. There was moss and you'd slip on the moss, and on the banks, little tracks would be going down and there'd be moss on it, and ferns, and there'd be logs down where trees had fallen in. We used to use those, but you had to be careful when you stood up on them because they'd be slippery from the moss, and then you'd dive in and you could swim around underneath and open your eyes. The water was like silk. You could open your eyes. And the reeds in the bottom had moss on them and they also had little oxygen bubbles. You could see them. The white man has fucked it up now. Believe you me, it was heaven. I think to myself now, that was how they kept Australia for all those years and years and centuries before occupation, and here we've had 200 years and what's happened? Look at our rivers. How can you have pride in something like that.

Back to Strathfield

But I didn't last long there. They sent me back from Moonacullah, and I had stone bruises on my feet, so I couldn't wear shoes. I had on an old grey overcoat, so it must have been winter. And lo and behold, we walk into the old Aborigines Welfare Board building with the marble floors, down there in Bridge Street and there is Mrs Q waiting to greet me and forgive me and take me home again, and have a hot bath, have my feet looked after. One of the nicest things about going back there was getting between clean sheets. I had missed that, but didn't realise until I came back to it.

But of course our relationship fell to pieces again, I kept running away looking for my mother, so I was put into the Girl's Shelter. I was not going to settle down and accept what these people were trying to make me do. Finally I was charged with being uncontrollable and I was sent to Parramatta.

Parramatta Girls Home

They put me in Parramatta Girls Home. They said I was uncontrollable. I kept on running away, looking for my mother. Everywhere they put me from the age of about seven I'd be looking for her. I didn't run away to be naughty. I'm sure I didn't do it to be

My story begins ...

The Industrial School for Girls at Parramatta (Parramatta Girls Home)

The aim of the Industrial School was the moral improvement of young women: ' ... to take in hand the girls, who through defective parental oversight or from other causes have foolishly started on the wrong path'.

The Parramatta Girls Home was originally a Roman Catholic Orphan School established in 1841. In 1886 the NSW Government took over the grounds and a high perimeter wall was built. The next year the Governor of NSW declared that the land should be set apart as an Industrial School for Females. The *Neglected Children and Juvenile Offenders Act* of 1905 led to an emphasis on 'training and education as means of developing acceptable behaviour'. In 1912 the hospital section of the School became known as the Girl's Training Home and then the Girl's Industrial School. It was intended for 'girls of an uncontrollable character, but not of immoral tendencies'.

In 1946, under the *Child Welfare Act* of 1939, the School was renamed the Parramatta Training School for Girls, dedicated to 'the reception, detention, maintenance, discipline, education and training of young persons committed to such institutions'. It was intended as 'a home for destitute and vagrant girls, but in practice it was a reformatory for delinquents, [and] operated rather like a prison'. After major riots in 1961, the most difficult girls were sent to a new Institution for Girls at Hay. Parramatta Training School was phased out in 1974.

Source: Wharton 1911:128; NSW Government Gazette, 1912(1):769; 1946(2):1847; wwww.parragirls.org.au

naughty. I'd just think, 'I might go and see if I can find her.' I used to take myself off to all different places and that sort of thing.

I would have gone mad. But I managed to escape from there a few times. By this time escaping was becoming an adventure. Just running to get away from them.

I hated them. There is no other word. A child is very sensitive to feelings, to attitudes towards them. I may have been a bit more sensitive than others. But I knew they despised me. I found in my

Above: The old Parramatta Girls Home. It is largely unchanged from Nancy's day although it is now used for administration purposes only. Photo: Gaynor Macdonald (2002).

Left: The high wall of Parramatta Girls Home could be scaled to provide access to the creek and park beyond. Photo: Gaynor Macdonald (2002).

My story begins ...

The remains of one of the back gates. In 2002, Nancy pointed out the small trap door, now covered with weeds. This was one way the girls would try to escape. Photo: Gaynor Macdonald (2002).

papers, 'We feel this family has regretted taking a member of such a despised race into their home.' I couldn't believe that shit when I read it. I hadn't been wrong as a child. I was lucky getting my papers because it helped me come to terms with what I'd done as a child. When I read all that bullshit that's in my papers, I thought, 'That's why I did it.' They didn't have a clue. They didn't take the time to find out. I hated them. I hated the whites. And we Koori girls knew they hated us. They called us these dreadful names, gin, lubra. One girl, she did have fairly thick lips, and the superintendent used to call her 'Lubra Lips'.

It could be a very cruel place. Some of them were very vindictive, sadistic almost. The superintendent was a very cruel man. The kids gave him the nickname of Fritz. Everybody had a nickname. Fritz was a Kaiser. It was during the war or just after the war and, of course, instead of calling him 'the German' we called him Fritz. He would punch you and knock you down. And nothing was ever done about it. People would never believe you when you'd say something. It was like a gaol.

They just didn't believe what you said. They did not believe you. I bet there's not one thing written about them being cruel to us and punching us. They used to get us up in the middle of the night and they had this big covered way. It was all concrete and it had a big cover across it and it went from one set of buildings to another set of buildings. And for punishment we used to have to scrub it with a toothbrush. On punishment nights he'd drag us out of bed in our nightdresses, which were cotton calico, and we'd go down and stand one at the posts and one between the posts, one at the post and one between the posts, like that right down to the end. There was a girl we used to call Chook, because she used to make chook noises. I'll never forget her. She went crrrrrrrr when he walked past, and he was nearly up to the top where he used to stand. He spun around, 'Who did that, who did it?' And everybody stepped forward. Everybody stepped forward. We knew he would have half killed her, everybody had to step out. He was such a cruel man.

You worked from the minute you got up, to the minute you went to bed. We worked in the laundry. We used to do sheets for the hospital and I think for the mental hospital. They had these great big coppers and they'd be filled with boiling water and sheets. You had to lift them out with these copper sticks onto these big sort of cages, like shopping trolleys, and then you had to wheel them over to a big tub full of water. Then you had to lift them out into that tub and rinse them, and then you'd have to lift them out again. Then they'd let the water out and then you'd have to put the blue in. Outside down behind the hedge were all the lines. You had to go and peg them all down along the lines.

Upstairs in the laundry, where you can look up at the panes of glass in those photos we've got, was the top of the laundry. Up there was where the soap used to go in. It was put into blocks like bars of soap to dry. When they first arrived they were very soft. They'd wait until the blocks got dry and then they'd get you to cut them. I think it used to come from the prison or somewhere like that. This big lot of soap would come in and we'd have to put one this way and one that way and build them up and they'd dry. Why on earth they didn't get us to cut it while it was new and soft I don't know. And I'd have blisters on my hands from cutting this soap. We used to stand up and look out the panes of the windows and you could see down to the river near where the crossing is going over, and we used to look down and see people playing down there and watch them. I wasn't very happy there. I don't think anybody was.

But that's where I met Bessie, she was one of the women who got me interested in singing. She taught me to sing Ave Maria in Latin. I can still remember all these songs that she taught me. She used to say, 'Nance, you have a beautiful voice. You have a beautiful voice.' She used to play and she had a big thick book with all songs in it, and she used to teach me all the songs from that. We did Shakespearean plays and that's when I got interested in that sort of thing.

My favourite person there was Miss H. I just adored her. Adored her! And when she had a day off my days were miserable, because I focussed all my love and attention onto her, in my life. She treated me with a lot of respect and I suppose wanting a mother so badly and not having one, that she was the ideal substitute. She was very good to me. She used to say, 'Can Nancy come up and clean my room for me?' So I'd go up, and it wouldn't need cleaning and she'd have a cup of tea made. 'Come and sit down and we'll have a talk,' she'd say. Just to get me away from it. I think it was the love of Miss H that kept me sane. She was my lifeline. I would thank God when the note came down. She seemed to know when I was stressed. The note would come down, that she needed me to scrub the wall or something. She was lovely, bloody beautiful.

I kept in touch with her all those years. And even after all those years, when Megan and David were little I rang her up, I used to ring her up, and she said, bring your kids down. She lived down near the Catholic Monastery in Dulwich Hill, in Challis Avenue. And I went around to see her and she hadn't changed. And she loved Megan and David. I would say, 'Behave yourselves!' They were doing exactly what I didn't want them to do. She'd tell me not to worry. I thanked her for what she had done and told her what she meant to me. She was like my substitute mother. Horsey they all called her. That was her nickname, Horsey H. She was lovely.

The only time you ever went out was if you'd been behaving and you'd go on the back of a truck in these khaki shorts and tops down to Bobbin Head for the day. And that was great. I used to say to the kids, I don't care who you run away from, but you don't run away from Horsey. Nobody runs away, because I'll come after you. I knew that old superintendent 'Fritz' used to really go after the staff if any of the kids got away. And I can remember one Sunday they got away. She was a Catholic and she was taking the kids to St Patrick's Church and about four or five of them took off. I said, 'I'll go and get them.' I went with the superintendent and I caught them, well, two or three of them anyway. And of course they said I was a traitor. And I said, 'I don't give a stuff, I told you before you did it. If you do that to her then watch out.' They never tried it again. She was a good woman. She was just so good, good to the kids.

From Parramatta to Callan Park

There were six of us. We were all in Parramatta Girls Home. We were in there, in trouble for something, and in there they had a cell block. Six cells. Locked. The walls were painted green and blotched with red – if you weren't a South Sydney's supporter you were in for a bit of trouble! Over the light they had a cage type thing. The table was fixed to the wall. The seat was fixed to the floor. And you sat in there all day without a blanket or anything.

Depending on your crime you either spent 24, 48, or 72 hours in there. I think we must have been the 72 mob that were in there because we'd done something, I dunno what, probably smoked. If you smoked they'd put you in there. If you gave them cheek they'd put you in there. Not doing your work properly. Minor things. Now, when I see what the kids do today, my God! But you'd be in there and you'd sit there all day, bored shitless. I mean there's no other word for it. And you'd be talking to each other and you'd be lying on the floor. This is why I have arthritis now so badly. I'm sure of it. You could call out when you got down near the door, on the floor. And in the morning they'd take you out one at a time and you could have a cold

My story begins ...

Callan Park

The Callan Estate, covering 104.5 acres, was purchased by the Colonial Government of New South Wales in 1873 to establish a large 'lunatic asylum' which was called the Hospital for the Insane, Callan Park (ODC 1990). Originally a branch of the Gladesville Mental Hospital, it became a separate institution for the 'care and control of the insane' in 1878 (McClements 1961:53). In the mid 1900s, Callan Park Hospital was the subject of a number of Royal Commissions and inquiries (ODC 1990). In 1961, a Royal Commission found that it was in serious need of reform, identified as 'basically a problem of Medical, Community and Governmental attitudes; the defects of accommodation, medical and nursing care, food and clothing are but symptomatic of something more fundamental' (McClements 1961:33):

'Callan Park is heir to a tradition that you place patients in one mould; that you gear therapy to a system of locked wards; that you do not give patients food because it will not be appreciated; that you do not clothe them well because they will wet their clothes and dirty them or spill food on them; a tradition that you do not put doors on bathrooms or WCs because some patients will use these places as a means of suicide or to indulge in indecent acts; that you disallow privacy in their sleeping accommodation because they cannot be overseen; a tradition that you refuse them liberty because a man might seduce a woman patient, run away or do some other harm.'

At the time of this Royal Commission, Callan Park accommodated 1743 patients (McClements 1961:53). There were only six females between 15–20 years of age in a total of 563. Patients were classified into wards as workers, refractory, chronic dements, chronic troublesome, hospital or open (McClements 1961:55–56).

shower. One little shower in the yard. But you weren't even allowed to walk around there. As soon as you washed yourself and dried yourself and everything and rolled your bed up and plonked it down, then you were put back in the cell.

So we all decided that we'd had enough of this, life must be greener on the other side, so we decided to bump ourselves off. Just before Chook comes in for the evening to give us our beds, we'll all swing ourselves off the light, holding on, and as she's opening the door we'll let go. But it wasn't so risky because as soon as you let go and took the full weight of this cage thing around the light, it fell down. And you'd lie there and you go, ck-ck-ck-ck (sort of choking noises). Well, we did this and wasn't she in a flip. She's screaming out for the superintendent. So here we were, all committing suicide.

We all got sent to the Reception House which was in Darlinghurst behind the old jail there, where the old police station was, down behind there. All six of us were sent in there. It was wonderful! They had wonderful food, lying in a beautiful bed all day, nurses spoiling us. See I knew what it'd be like because I'd been sent there before. My foster parent had sent me there because I was vague and she thought I might have had a brain tumour. That's another story.

It was called the Reception House where they decided what to do with you - either you were going to be certified or you weren't. We decided we were going to be certified. We weren't going to be sent back to Parramatta. So there was Dorothy, I remember her, 'Googie Withers' she was called because she had lice in her hair when she came in and she had to have a big bow on her head, so she got the name of 'Googie'. We all got certified. 'Insane'. So some of us got sent to Gladesville, some of us got sent to Callan Park.

Callan Park

I went to Callan Park. It was wonderful! Absolutely wonderful! The food was better. We were treated much better. We were treated as patients and we had to be looked after. When we got there the nurses used to spoil you, like this Fran. She lives down in Caringbah now, she wrote me this beautiful letter after I spoke at Parliament House. 'Are you the same Nancy?' 'Yes, I am.' I rang her up.

The nurse that wrote to me said she always thought that I was different, that I wasn't nutty, 'cos I always had a code of honour. I would clear out all the time. She said, you were always running away, getting out, escaping. It was all a big game to me. But I would never do it when she took me out. She said, 'You always had the opportunity but you never did it. You had an honour system within yourself that you didn't even consider it.'

My story begins ...

Because I used to shoot through all the time, they stuck me up in the refractory ward, which was the worst type of mental patients. In those days, mental patients wore usually 'straightjackets' the whole time. Day and night, and they used to come out of their beds and they were put on these stools that used to go backwards and forwards and then they were tied onto that.

I can still think of some funny things that happened. The toilet was a hole in the wall. It was in the dormitory, a hole with a toilet in it, no door. Anyway you'd sit on that and the chain was in a bit of jute, and that would come down and you'd only have as much chain that you could pull, so you wouldn't hang yourself on the chain. And I remember, I never forget a name, her name was Hook. She'd be sitting in her jacket and she'd be sitting up and watching all this and see she kept jumping up and pulling the chain before you'd got off! She'd say,

The Bidura Children's Home, Glebe in 2001. Photo: Mervyn Bishop.

'That's the way, wash their arse for them.'

I don't know how long I was in Callan Park. I ended up having shock treatment. They also put me on some drug that made me so dopey. They gave you a gag to bite, you were on your back and they'd put the pillow under the small of your back, hold onto you and boom! And of course you wouldn't remember it. One day it went wrong. They didn't knock me out. I could feel all the electricity going through my body. Terrifying it was. I think they used the shock treatment to try and quieten you down. It was pretty terrifying. Do you know the next day they came and got me and held me down and gave it to me again. And they knew how stuffing terrified I was. I was terrified of electricity for years after. I never told anybody about that but it was horrible. It was horrible. And to be locked up with all these people, not one bit of sense was coming out of them. And they'd be walking, they did a lot of walking, up and down, and not slowly, real energetic. It wasn't long after that that the lobotomies came in. Thank God they didn't give me one of those!

Bloomfield

Then they decided to move me up to Bloomfield. They said, we'll put her up there and she won't know how to run away. But of course there's no high walls up there. It's a completely different atmosphere altogether. But we still got up to mischief. And I met other Koori girls.

We had an Irish nurse there who was a stuck up bitch. I couldn't stand her. We found a blue tongue lizard and it was the most docile thing. We stuck it on the mat and then we watched through the window. And she came back from lunch, she was singing, and sort of moving her head, I can still see her. She got her key out, and looks at her key to open the gate. Then she spots this lizard. Well, you can imagine what happened. She went berserk. And of course, we were killing ourselves laughing, never let on that we knew it was there.

I found security in having my day ordered for me. It was an easy life. I wasn't expected to work, and you had three good meals a day, good clean bed to sleep in, you had hot showers, entertainment, pictures, dances, picnics, I mean you had everything. Why would you give that up? I met a wonderful doctor there who knew that I was not insane.

Another story ...
the written record

Bloomfield marked the end of Nancy's life under the control of the Child Welfare Department. Before she continues with her story, we turn to the 'other story' of her childhood, the one told in the files kept by the Child Welfare Department on these same years.

Much later in her life, Nancy was able to access her file from the Child Welfare Department. It is hard to imagine what it must have been like for her to read these records. It is possible to read every page and seldom be aware that this is the life of a young child being recorded. There is no intimacy or affection. There is no record of Nancy's pain. The papers are confronting in their lack of sensitivity and humanity, very different to the records of a child's life that a parent would keep. These records reveal much about the Child Welfare Department's own approach to its role as guardian.

As a bureaucratic story it is, as might be expected, patchy and partial. It unfolds slowly, as events cause this child to become, from time to time, an object of bureaucratic concern and cause for a file note. Sometimes she merely needs medical or dental attention, or a foster parent wants their bills paid. One glimpses a sense of frustration on the part of Department officials now and then, such as when a foster parent requires this child to be moved yet again. Very rarely are questions asked about anything other than Nancy's material welfare.

The story intensifies as Nancy enters her teens, as she becomes more able to articulate her own distress. While from time to time one can glimpse sympathetic concern for Nancy, even if rarely in meaningful ways, the file comments can also be appalling – such as when she is assessed as being capable only of housework by someone who clearly recognised her abilities, or is accused of lying when she brings uncomfortable problems to those supposed to care for her.

One thing that stands out from this file is that few people talked to Nancy herself. Some foster mothers were able to get close but these relations were not sustained. Neither the files nor Nancy explain why. One mother tried consistently to assist Nancy but it seems she was prompted more by her sense of Christian duty than her love of her foster daughter. One official, when Nancy was admitted to the Girls' Industrial Home at Parramatta at the age of 14, took time to really listen to Nancy but this woman's insights

One life, two stories

Nancy and Jane working on Nancy's records in Gaynor's office, 2001. Photo: Gaynor Macdonald.

and recommendations were not acted on in any meaningful way. Nancy recalls that she often felt like a number. Indeed, for much of her life she was just that: a file number for the Child Welfare Department and, while at the Parramatta Girls Home, Number 26.

These were decades in Australian life in which children were often seen but not heard. They were seldom regarded as people in their own right, with their own credible opinions, and capable of insights into their own behaviour. Nancy was observed rather than spoken with. When she spoke out, she was ignored or accused of lying. Nancy had considerable difficulty dealing with the inconsistencies and finicky ways of one foster mother, whom even the Child Welfare Department recognised as very erratic, but the Department still left Nancy with her.

In the 1940s it was quite common for both Aboriginal and white children to be deemed uncontrollable. It is also clear that the Department accepted the claims of foster parents that Nancy was a difficult rebellious trouble-maker or that she lied without checking with Nancy herself, such as when her claims to being sexually assaulted were ignored. Many children think about and do 'run away from home' – most, fortunately, go just down the road, as in Nancy's case. But most are not consigned to a detention centre as a result.

Nancy was defined as uncontrollable by foster parents long before she was formally charged with being 'uncontrollable' under the *Child Welfare Act* and the *Aborigines Protection Act*. But her records make it clear that 'uncontrollable' often meant no more than not fitting in or not meeting other people's expectations. It stemmed from the number of times that she ran away. But by the time she was in her mid-teens, she had given it more substance. Nancy's file increases significantly with the reports produced in her final years 'in care', with police intervention and many court appearances. No one knew what to do with her – and it often seemed as if Nancy didn't know either.

Nancy describes these years of her life as being desperately unhappy. She describes her teenage years as the most confusing and dreadful time: ten desperate years when there was nobody in this world who cared about her. She was constantly feeling as if she did not belong anywhere.

The files indicate a spiralling life, spinning ever faster out of control. It is a story of increasing loneliness, increasing alienation from a real world of home, friends, school and neighbours. It would be a much longer journey before Nancy worked out how to belong for herself.

Nancy was caught in a complex web of inequality and powerlessness which combined her status as child with that of being Aboriginal, further complicated by her gender. These were social disadvantages in mid-twentieth century Australia that even her high IQ could not combat.

At the end of this chapter, we have provided a 'timeline' to help you follow Nancy's story. It lists the 'homes' that Nancy was in over her first 18 years although it does not include all the stays in the Bidura Children's Home between placements. In her teens, the stays between institutional transfers were in the Shelter of the Metropolitan Children's Court (the Shelter) rather than Bidura.

Nancy's 'official file' story

The files say little about Nancy until she was six years old. She was born in Crown Street Hospital, Sydney, on 11 March 1932. It seems she was with her mother for about 13 or 14 months before she was taken into state care and fostered out for the first time in early May 1933. In September of that year she contracted whooping cough.

Her first foster mother, Mrs A in Merrylands, later claimed she cared for Nancy until she was six but the records show that she was moved two times before her sixth birthday, with a stay at the Bidura Children's Home in between. The records say she was moved from this first home because she was 'sexually promiscuous' – whatever that means when a child is five years old. In fact, Nancy remembers this home fondly. It is where the only picture she now has of her entire childhood was taken, probably when she

One life, two stories

Nancy with her foster brother, when she was about four and a half or five years old. The only photo she had of her life until she was in her fifties. Photographer unknown.

was about three and a half or four years old. She is playing with her foster brother. Nancy also started school while living at Merrylands.

Fostering is a transitory, elusive relationship. One minute you are family, the next you can be moved on. In her second foster home in Marrickville, her foster mother soon became ill and had to be hospitalised for an operation, so she asked for Nancy to be moved. Foster children are expected to move in situations for which conventional families would have to find solutions that did not involve 'giving back' a child.

Nancy's third foster home was in Arncliffe. But she only stayed six months before being taken back to Bidura. Nancy remembers waiting with her foster mother on Arncliffe Station. She noticed her red bonnet in her foster mother's handbag, and knew she was being sent away again. At Bidura she was paraded before Mrs M from Willoughby, who became her fourth foster mother.

In July 1938, Mrs M wrote to the Child Welfare Department wanting more information about Nancy, then aged six, because she was 'required to manage many problems and many to overcome ... to help myself also the child' [sic]. Her concern suggests that, by then, Nancy was becoming thoroughly unsettled, frightened and insecure. This was to be compounded by her stay in this home – this was the house in which Nancy was living

Another story ...

when she was raped. As she tells in her own story, her foster mother's response was hostile. When Nancy told her what had happened to her – she was a child of 7 years by then – she was accused of lying. Her foster mother took a knife from the kitchen drawer and threatened to cut her tongue out if she told anyone.

All it says in the official record is that the foster mother returned Nancy without notice to the Bidura Children's Home in January 1940 and sent the following letter to the Child Welfare Department:

Mrs M, 30 January 1940, Chatswood

Dear Sir

I had occasion to return state ward Nancy Edwards to Bidura Church Home Glebe today, my efforts have been totally in vain, I tried for 2 years to give the child a chance in the world and am sorry and dissapointed at failing the problems are too many and too strong for me.

Respectively yours

[punctuation and spelling has been left as in originals for this and all the following correspondence and reports.]

Nancy was then sent to a family in Bankstown where she only stayed eight months before the foster mother asked for her transfer.

Mrs S, 8 September 1940, Bankstown

With regard to Nancy Edwards who has been boarding with me for about eight months, I find it advisable to return her to the Department. Unfortunately it seems impossible for her to adapt herself to our way, despite a large amount of patience, over a long period she shows no response.

Nancy, by then eight years old, went to Strathfield to Mrs P's family, where she stayed for some years, attending school in South Strathfield. It seems it was not an easy relationship between foster mother and foster child. Moments of affection alternated with hostility and distrust – on both sides. This was the house where Nancy was beaten because she had 'taught their daughter to lie.' Nancy also recalls that this daughter was quite put out by Nancy's presence in the family. Nevertheless, she became fond of her foster father and foster brother. Desperately unhappy, she says herself that she became more and more rebellious. Nancy recalls that, when she was ten years old, she tried to commit suicide and soon after that ran away for the first time. Nancy recalls the police finding her sound asleep in a telephone box.

One life, two stories

The police record is semi-legible but appears to recognise that, although Nancy had been recognised as being 'a little difficult', her foster mother was seen as 'intolerant of childish faults' and the subsequent Child Welfare report commented that 'Most of these are childish pranks which should have been forgotten long ago.'

1943

Nancy Edwards, aged 10 [in fact she had turned 11]

Notes on file: Nancy Edwards was forbidden to go to her school sports, as a penalty for lying and disobedience. She attended the sports, saying her teachers pushed her into the lines and marched off. Later, afraid to return home after disobedience, she used a penny she had to pay her fares to a former guardian in Bankstown. Leaving this person's home at about 5.30 pm having no money to travel with, she wandered aimlessly about the shopping centres of Bankstown, until found by the police ...

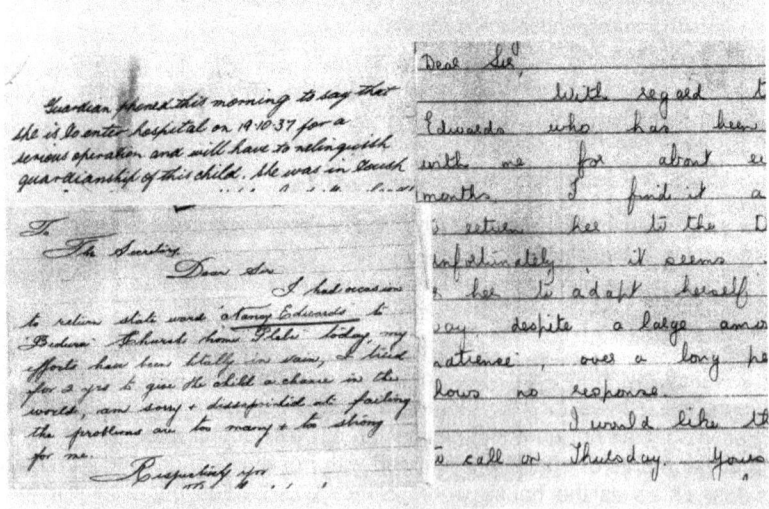

Things can't have been easy for foster parents either in these days. They also had to operate under the regulations of the Child Welfare Department. Foster parents had to go to lengths not normally required of parents – for instance in obtaining quotations for medical and dental treatment. On one occasion, one of Nancy's foster parents was instructed

Another story ...

to get a third quotation, as in the first two, 'neither of the quotations was very satisfactory'. In the meantime, one can only wonder how Nancy was dealing with one tooth that needed extracting and seven that required fillings (Dept of Education to Child Welfare Department B4867, 28 Dec 1943).

Nancy's first foster mother, Mrs A, kept in touch with her. In December 1943 she wrote to the Child Welfare Department asking for permission to visit Nancy at the home of her present foster parents. She notes in her letter, 'I am interested in her and she would like to be able to come to see us again. Mrs P asked me to write and get permission for Nancy to come here or go out with us occasionally.' This permission was granted. Nancy recalls that when she was about ten years old, she ran away from the P family and went back to the A family, her first foster home, looking for her mother.

Nancy was with the P family in Strathfield from September 1940 to January 1944 but she also ran away several other times. Both she and her foster mother seem to have been content for her to be returned. Nevertheless, the records indicate that her foster mother's own behaviour and attitudes continued to be erratic.

It is frequently recorded on Nancy's file that she was a very bright child. Correspondence from Mrs P 18 January 1944 to the Child Welfare Department records that 'she was proved by a test that was given in October 1940 when it was stated that at that time she had the intelligence of 11 years, although only 8 years old.'

In 1944, when she was almost 12 years old, Nancy started high school at Burwood Secondary School. She wanted a school uniform, wanted to be like the other girls, to fit in, but the Child Welfare Department responded to her foster mother's request by saying that uniforms were 'not insisted on' because of the war. However, they relented and arranged for her to obtain one.

The Child Welfare Department report of 9 March 1944 notes that, after running off yet again, Nancy had now settled down and was attending school. There is 'every reason to believe that she will again become happy and contented in her usual surroundings'. But only a week later, she was off again. This time she told the Department she didn't want to stay with Mrs P any longer and they didn't send her back. Their problem was what to do next.

Nancy was held on remand in Bidura until arrangements were made for the Church Missionary Society (CMS) to look after her, 'with a view to forwarding her ambition to become a medical missionary' (Child Welfare Department, B4867, 13 April 1944). She was taken to Mulgoa, a 'half caste settlement' outside Penrith in western Sydney that CMS ran on behalf of the Federal Government.

However, CMS staff were concerned at what they saw as an inappropriate placement:

CMS, 5 May 1944

This child, however, is of High School age, and we would prefer that she should be in the metropolitan area so that she might attend a High School, and develop the undoubted intellectual ability which she possesses.

On the 5th May, 1944, Nancy was sent to her seventh foster family, Mr and Mrs F, arranged by the CMS, at Eastwood. From there she briefly attended Hornsby Domestic Science School. She ran away twice from this placement, although no reasons were ever reported.

During this time, Nancy's previous foster mother, Mrs P, had kept in touch with her through letters, and with the permission of the new foster mother. In June 1944, Mrs P wrote to the Child Welfare Department:

Mrs P to Child Welfare Department, 25 June 1944

Nancy still being interested in us – no, more – still loving us – she has always been most affectionate and loving towards us ... I have heard from Mrs F that things are not going well with Nancy at school. Maybe you will be able to set things right.

Things were not just a problem at school. This was the home in which Nancy was sexually assaulted for the second time. Obviously, as she recounted, this was an extremely distressing experience for Nancy. But once again her distress went unheard. No one asked why she had run away twice from this home. It was documented in the records that Nancy had been going to neighbours telling lies about the foster family that were of 'an embarrassing nature.' Obviously, no one believed the good Reverend would abuse a child.

In July the CMS sent her back to Bidura. Life was about to change quite dramatically.

From foster care to institutional care

By now Nancy was thoroughly conversant with Bidura, appropriately known as 'the depot', and it was indeed more of a depot for processing children than a Children's Home. Here Nancy met up with other girls whose lives were very unsettled, with life experiences very similar to Nancy's. It is the friends that Nancy made during these stays, and later in the Parramatta Girls Home, that came to mean more to her through her life than those encountered through foster homes and schools. But this visit was to mark a defining moment in Nancy's life.

Another story ...

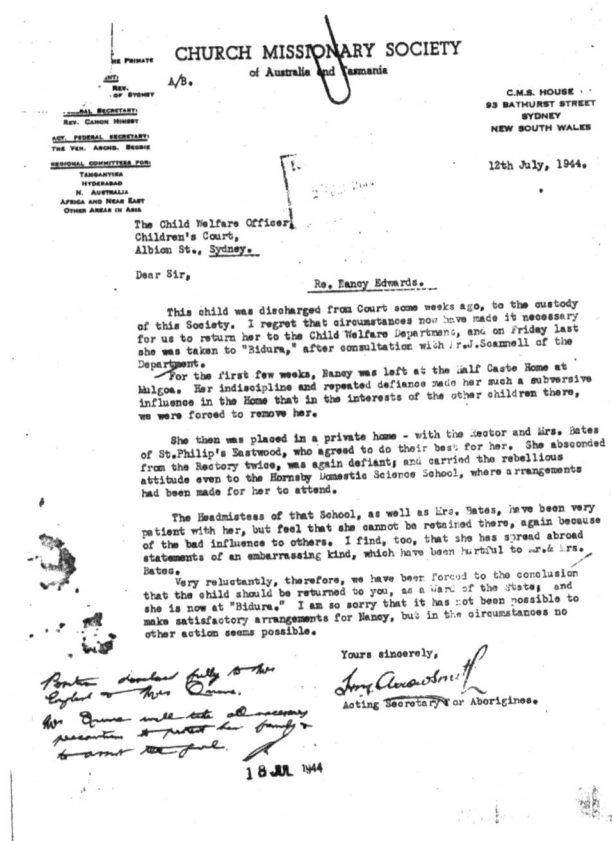

At Sydney on 13 July 1944, the Metropolitan Children's Court found that 'Nancy May Edwards, is an uncontrollable child within the meaning of the *Aborigines Protection Act*, 1901–1940.'

She was remanded until 14 July 1944, and on the 18 July was committed to the care of the Aborigines Welfare Board, to be dealt with as a ward of the Court. This was not the end of foster homes but it was the beginning of the Child Welfare Department's focus on institutional care facilities rather than private homes as a way of placing Nancy. She was twelve years old.

On 14 December, the Aborigines Welfare Board sent Nancy to their Aboriginal Girls Training Home in Cootamundra, more commonly known as the Cootamundra Girls' Home. This move was perhaps to see if Nancy would be more settled in an Aboriginal environment but Cootamundra was also not a particularly appropriate placement and it is hardly surprising that the staff there soon reported that Nancy's behaviour was 'unsatisfactory'. It was noted in the reports of this time that Nancy was a bad influence on the other children, continually escaping and challenging authority.

The Board then sent her to Moonacullah in February 1945. This was Nancy's first stay with an Aboriginal family and Nancy obviously valued this time immensely. But it seemed to bring into starker relief the way in which Nancy was now caught between worlds, not able to find acceptance or a meaningful world among either white people or Aboriginal people – although she clearly experienced the people of Moonacullah as accepting and as people she could identify with. However, it seems that someone didn't believe she was 'fitting in'. Her stay, with all its rich memories, was short-lived. Nancy was given a little taste of being with Aboriginal people and then removed again.

Mrs P wrote in July 1945 to again ask if Nancy could be transferred to her care. She was obviously distressed at Nancy's association with Aboriginal people – it is little wonder that Nancy herself was becoming increasing confused and upset.

Mrs P, 6 July 1945, Strathfield

About 3 months ago I wrote you concerning Nancy Edwards, a ward of A.W.B. Some 3 weeks later, I received a reply stating that your department was endeavouring to get Nancy onto a farm, failing that my offer would be considered. This is just a reminder in case the matter might have slipped your memory.

I fear if Nancy is left too long in her present place she may deteriorate to the level of the poor creatures whom she associates with. In view of past experience I am not sure that our home is the ideal place, as I think she felt the need of a companion nearer her own age. We are quite willing, however, to try again. A Church home might be good. That is just a suggestion.

I did not write to Nancy while she was in Cootamundra. When she arrived at Moonacullah she wrote me. I have marked the letter (1). You can read the appeal in the words of the songs. That is Nancy's way of saying she is sorry. I answered her letter.

After that her letters were bright. Lately they are becoming quiet, as if she is losing hope.

She is thirteen years old and needs a mother's care. After all she has not done anything very dreadful. It would be nice if she could have another chance

Another story ...

somewhere. If she needed a lesson, surely six months on an aboriginal station ought to be sufficient. A trial would not make much difference to anyone.

After all but for an accident of birth any of us might have been in the same position. I am enclosing letters, which give you an idea how Nancy feels. Would you please put them in the enclosed stamped envelope and return, as I value them.

I do hope you will excuse this second letter.

Nancy was moved from Moonacullah. The next Child Welfare Department file entry has her in Dalmar Children's Home in Carlingford, northwestern Sydney, but this was also a short stay. It was about this time that the Aboriginal Welfare Board Superintendent suggested she be returned to Mrs P if both Nancy and Mrs P agreed.

It is possible that Nancy also absconded from Dalmar because on 19 September 1945 she was once again remanded to the Metropolitan Girls Shelter (the Shelter). However, she recalls being back with the P family when the war ended in September.

Nancy, then 13 years old, was taken to Court on 8 October 1945 where she was 'committed to an Institution' – the Parramatta Industrial School for Girls, also known as the Parramatta Girls Home – on the charge of being 'Uncontrollable'. On her committal form her IQ is recorded as 125. The testing Clinic's recommendation was for the 'stable discipline and routine of an institution until adolescence passed'. The Court determined: 'She is of violent disposition and it is desired that she be moved direct from the Court to the Institution'. However, despite this statement there is no evidence at this time or at any other time that Nancy was 'violent' towards either people or her surroundings. However, she did by then use what was described as 'filthy language' which may have been alarming enough in a young teenager in the 1940s.

Nancy did go out to Parramatta Girls Home but the next day, 9 October, she was admitted to the Infectious Diseases Division of Prince Henry Hospital with scarlet fever. It is clear that she had been ill from at least 2 October and had already seen two different doctors before going to Court on 8 October.

After the ten days' quarantine period for scarlet fever, the hospital reported that Nancy was comfortable and doing well. Once well, she was transferred back to Parramatta.

On 31 October, Mrs P again wrote expressing her great concern, this time at the move of Nancy to a juvenile detention centre.

One life, two stories

Mrs P, Strathfield, 31 October 1945

Dear Sir

I am writing in reference to Nancy Edwards, a State Ward. Nancy was boarded out to us in Dec 1940. She lived with us as our foster child until Jan 1944. Since then we have had her with us at times, although she has been moved about quite a lot and has been in care of the Aborigines Welfare Board some of the time.

Nancy was admitted to the Industrial School for girls at Parramatta on 8th inst.

The girl is a problem, but as far as I know her, not bad. She is irresponsible and unreliable and anyone undertaking to help her must be prepared for this.

Nancy has another side however. She is affectionate and loving and I can honestly say, that the girl was never once rude, in her manner towards me during the time she lived in our home. Her intelligence is good.

Mr Y, will you look up the girl's history, and see whether there is anything you can do. Nancy is impressionable and easily led. What will the company at Parramatta School do to her? I have taught her carefully and painstakingly. What is going to happen to Nancy when she leaves the School? Will she be able to fit into ordinary normal home life? I am all for law and order, but the law can be very hard and impersonal. Has every avenue been tried wherein Nancy might be helped. If she were your child or my child, could something else be done.

Nancy is at present in Prince Henry hospital with scarlet fever. I have visited her there. She has promised me that she will be good at Parramatta, however, it is one thing to say that in the peaceful, pleasant atmosphere of the hospital, another to carry it out in the altogether different and most unsuitable atmosphere of the other place.

Well, Mr Y., I have made my appeal and must leave the matter there, except in prayer. Nancy is a quarter caste aboriginal.

I am, Yours truly

Mrs P wasn't going to leave it there. The following day, 1 November 1945, she also wrote to the Duchess of Gloucester, wife of the Governor General, in a similar vein, asking for intervention on Nancy's behalf. The Duchess's Secretary, Miss Horsey, responded the following week:

Secretary to Duchess of Gloucester, 8 November 1945, to Mrs P

I am directed by the Duchess of Gloucester to tell you that her Royal Highness much sympathises with your wish to help the part-aboriginal girl, Nancy

Another story ...

Edwards. The Duchess regrets that it is not possible for her to give you any direct assistance, but your letter will be forwarded to the appropriate Department for attention with a request that the notes you enclosed may be returned to you.

This correspondence was sent to the Premier's Department, who then forwarded it, marked 'Urgent', to the Child Welfare Department. Only after this did the Department, on 19 November, respond to Mrs P's letter of 31 October. They informed Mrs P that Nancy was currently in hospital and 'shortly she will be ready for transfer to the Girls' Industrial School at Parramatta for further training'. It does, however, ask Mrs P if she would be prepared to 'accept the care of Nancy when she is ready for discharge'.

In fact, Nancy had already been transferred back to Parramatta Girls Home on 14 November, five days previously, and only a week after major surgery. On 3 November, while Nancy was still in hospital recuperating from scarlet fever, she was diagnosed with appendicitis. She had an appendectomy on 7 November.

On Nancy's return to Parramatta, she 'behaved badly' and was sent to the Reception House in Darlinghurst on 18 November where she underwent testing. Evidently, the Child Welfare Department was now concerned for her mental health. However, the Medical Report dated 25 November 1945 stated: 'Nancy May Edwards is above average intelligence and whilst here has shown no sign of certifiable mental disorder.' The Department's letter had the notation, 'Girl is not certifiable. Will be returned this afternoon.' A footnote stated both parents were 'deceased'.

What stands out is that Nancy, with above average intelligence, received very inadequate schooling in the critical years she was in the Girls' Industrial Home in Parramatta. She was a passionate reader – and remained so all her life – and this was one way she sought comfort, as when she was at the Cootamundra Girls' Home. Her scholastic ability was confirmed by her later entry into university in her fifties. In her Aboriginal Studies major she obtained straight A grades. By then she had created for herself the environment of confidence and motivation she needed to develop her skills and interests – something her institutionalised childhood did not provide.

In the meantime, Mrs P had kept up her correspondence with the Department and had written again on 20 November. The file note indicates that an officer of the Department would call on her shortly to discuss her concerns about Nancy. On 14 December there is a report by an officer of his visit to Mrs P, recommending that Nancy be consulted about whether or not she wished to be returned to Mrs P. However, an Inspector's Report of 27 December at Parramatta recommended that the decision as to 'whether it would be of use returning Nancy to Mrs P' only be made after Nancy had been in the Institution for some time.

In April 1946 the Aborigines Welfare Board (AWB), who still had formal responsibility for Nancy, also suggested to the Child Welfare Department that Nancy 'now be given a further trial and placed in the care of some suitable white guardian, the girl to remain under the control of the Child Welfare Department in view of her very light caste'. (AWB, 9 May 1946). Again in June, the Aborigines Welfare Board wrote recommending that Nancy be returned to Mrs P, although it did note that Mrs P doubted she could get Nancy to go to school. Nevertheless, she was anxious, as was Nancy herself by this time, to have her return. The Board commented that Nancy would have more chance of success with Mrs P than with anyone else 'but that she must always be regarded as an extremely doubtful case' (AWB, 21 June 1946). The Child Welfare Department's response to the Board merely stated that the suggestion had been noted and that the Board would be notified when a decision had been reached.

Despite the file note stating Nancy's parents were deceased, it was at this time that serious attempts were at last made to try and locate them. On 2 January 1946, the Aboriginal Welfare Board wrote to the Parramatta Girls Home in response to a communication of 17 December 1945:

Aboriginal Welfare Board, 2 January 1946, to Parramatta Girls Home

Although extensive enquires have been made with a view to locating the mother of the above named girl, Ruby Josephine Edwards, it has not been possible to trace her whereabouts. Nothing is known of the child's father.

By now Mrs P was visiting Nancy at Parramatta regularly each fortnight. On 31 March 1946 she again wrote to the Aboriginal Welfare Board saying, 'I desire to inform you that our home is still open to Nancy should the Board still wish to place her with us.' Perhaps in response, the Board wrote to the Child Welfare Department the next day, 1 April 1946, but made no reference to Mrs P.

Acting Secretary, Aboriginal Welfare Board 1 April 1940, to Child Welfare Department

This girl's case received consideration at the meeting of the AWB held on 12th March last.

It will be remembered that this girl was a ward of the Child Welfare Department until July 1944, when she was committed to the care of the AWB. Nancy was permitted to return to the care of her former guardian Mrs P as a boarded out ward under the care of the AWB. She was very unsettled, however, and

Another story ...

eventually in December 1944 she was transferred to the Aboriginal Girls Training Home, Cootamundra. She did not settle down amongst the other dark girls at the home and in February, 1945, she was boarded out to an aboriginal family residing at the Aboriginal Station, Moonacullah, via Deniliquin. This arrangement did not prove satisfactory as Nancy, being accustomed to white people and their way of life, found it difficult to assimilate herself into the life of an Aboriginal Station.

Arrangements were subsequently made for the girl to be returned to Sydney and admitted to the Dalmar Children's Home, Church St, Carlingford. She absconded from the Institution and returned to the home of her former guardian, Mrs P, but she again gave trouble and on the 17th September she was brought before the Children's Court and committed as an uncontrollable child within the meaning of the Child Welfare Act, 1932-39, and transferred to Parramatta Industrial School for Girls.

Following a recent visit to Parramatta Home by a member of the Aborigines Welfare Board and a member of this Department, the Board gave consideration to this girl's case at its last meeting when it was directed that it be suggested that Nancy might now be given a further trial and placed in the care of some suitable white guardian but, in view of her very light caste, she should remain under the control of the Child Welfare Department.

As Nancy approaches the age when she can leave school, there is increasing concern on the part of welfare officials to identify what she could do once out of the care of the Department. She is given vocational tests, the results of which seem bizarre given her later accomplishments.

Vocational Report, Director of Youth Welfare, received by CWD 23 May 1946

Whilst it is possible that her test results may have been depressed through her present outlook and temperament, the trend suggests that Nancy would be most suited to those occupations where non-verbal factors and manipulative ability are of greater importance than capacity for verbal or theoretical training.

Her vocational interests are in nursing, and possibly missionary work. A position as a hospital wardsmaid should fulfil to some extent her interests in this direction. It is felt, in addition, that it would help towards Nancy's rehabilitation if she could be encouraged to study for the nurses' entrance examination: not only would this set a goal for her, but it would also tend to direct her energies along channels which have definite appeal for her.

Although it may appear that at the present moment Nancy is not temperamentally suited to nursing, placing such a goal before her should assist in establishing confidence in herself, through the realisation of her social acceptability, the lack of which may possibly have been the cornerstone of her maladjustment.

Should Nancy not settle down to a job as hospital wardsmaid, domestic or laundry work, kitchen maid, dress machining and finishing, glass etching, packing etc., are all suggested.

As happened on several occasions, these recommendations were not followed through. It seems that the Department took the line of least resistance – they eventually handed Nancy over to the care of Mrs P, but not immediately.

Acting Superintendent Industrial School for Girls, Parramatta, to CWD Director, 24 June 1946

Subject: The Case of Nancy Edwards, born 11.3.32.

Nancy Edwards has been a very difficult girl since her admission to the institution and has been involved in trouble on a number of occasions.

She has shown some improvement lately, possibly because many of the more troublesome girls have been absent from the institution, but she is still far from ready for discharge.

Mrs P has continued to show her interest in Nancy and writes and visits her regularly. Nancy appears to be attached to Mrs P and when ready for discharge will probably have more chance of success with Mrs P than if placed elsewhere.

It is recommended that Nancy should continue her training at this institution.

Mrs P persisted in her efforts as well, writing to the Department on 19 October 1946:

Mrs P to CWD, 19 October 1946

I wish to apply for guardianship of Nancy Edwards, a State Ward ... Her record [at the Parramatta Girls Home] has been, I understand, satisfactory for some time now.

The Department seems to have been reluctant to release Nancy into Mrs P's care again, concerned – rather too late in the day – for her education.

CWD Report, 11 November 1946

Mrs P has always indicated that she is prepared to take this girl on discharge. Nancy is attached to Mrs P, and the P home is the only stable part of her whole life.

Another story ...

I feel definitely when she is discharged, that she should go to Mrs P's home, although Nancy is so unstable, moody and peculiar in so many respects, that Mrs P will have a hard task ahead of her, but she is well aware of the situation, and will do her best to cope with it.

I feel very apprehensive, however, as to whether this girl will settle down back at school. She states she will go to school, but if she is discharged now, she will have to attend school for approx. one month, then have six weeks to do nothing in, and then have to return to school for at least two months.

If she is discharged, arrangements should be made as to which school she is to attend, as Nancy is most anxious not to go to any girls who might know her. Previously she attended the Burwood Home Science School, but her continued absence would make her very backward for ordinary academic work, but her high intelligence quota would probably preclude her from opportunity 7th work.

Recommendation: That when the girl is discharged, she should be discharged to the care of Mrs P, but that before discharge is contemplated the question of her schooling should be given careful consideration, as it will be of vital importance in Nancy's adjustment.

The Department's response to Mrs P on 28 November 1946 stated, 'consideration of the discharge of Nancy must be deferred until she attains the age of fifteen years and has had her tonsils removed'.

There is little privacy in the life of a state ward. Nancy's files record not only her medical history but continually revisit her 'status.' For instance, noted on a letter of 7 Nov 1946 regarding her 'unhealthy tonsils' is the additional comment: 'Girl was admitted to State Control on 8.5.33 on mother's application. She is an illegitimate child. Her mother has not been heard of since April 1934.'

There is no evidence of this 'application' on the part of Nancy's mother, or what circumstances might have led to it. What is evident is that Nancy's request to find out her mother's whereabouts become a persistent theme in the records. It is also around this time she enlisted the help of her first foster mother, Mrs A.

Letter from Mrs A (foster mother 1), Merrylands, 12 August 1946

Sir,

Nancy Edwards who is in the Girls Industrial School at Parramatta has written to me asking if I can tell her anything about her mother, who is Ruby Edwards. I had Nancy in my care from when she was 13 months old until she was six. Would it be possible to send me the address of Ruby Edwards somewhere in Pyrmont. I gave it to the Inspector from this district many years ago now and have no record of it. Nancy is very anxious to find her mother and I thought I may be able to help her.

Thanking you,

Yrs Faithfully,

The Child Welfare Department responded on 9 September 1946, giving Mrs A the 'last known address' they had for Ruby Edwards.

The end of childhood

Nancy was now fifteen years old and the issue of what to do next introduced a new agenda. When Mrs P visited her in January 1947 she suggested to Nancy that she become a ward maid instead of returning to school.

These discussions seem to have been put on hold for a while because Nancy had to have a tonsillectomy in the Parramatta District Hospital on 29 January but what kind of work Nancy would do had become a major concern for the Department. Coincidentally, when Nancy had her tonsillectomy she recalled that Mrs A's daughter was in charge of the ward.

Girls Industrial School, Parramatta, 15 January 1947

Mrs P seems a sensible understanding woman who is fond of Nancy. She seems to be able to understand Nancy's own particular problems and makes every effort to do her best for her. The home is clean and comfortable with a well kept garden. Mrs P said that she had visited Nancy on 11-1-47 and Nancy seemed anxious to return to school for another year, but Mrs P had tactfully suggested that it would be better for her to ... [illegible] ... work as a ward maid at Western Suburbs Hospital. I told Mrs P that I had seen Nancy on 14-1-47 and she seemed to have changed her mind and now wanted a job as a ward maid. Mrs P was very pleased that Nancy was now contemplating a position as a ward maid but she asked me if the Dept would make arrangements for her employment. She is quite prepared to make the arrangement herself but would rather the Dept did so. Mrs P would rather Nancy hadn't a sleeping out position but is agreeable to Nancy sleeping out if necessary.

CWD Report 14 February 1947

Question of this girl's employment has been discussed with Nancy continuously. She is the type of girl who needed a lot of help whilst in the Institution, and many hours have been spent with Nancy discussing her many problems and worries. She is particularly keen to do nursing, and from the Youth Welfare report, it would appear quite suitable. I have not seen Mrs P for sometime, ...

Another story ...

she desires us to find the girl employment. I do not consider it any use finalising employment until after the girl is discharged.

The day before her fifteenth birthday, on 10 March 1947, Nancy was finally discharged from the Parramatta Girls Home and released to the custody of Mrs P.

Despite all the discussions about her employment, when Nancy started work the next day it was at G J Coles' shop in Burwood. This was not an option she had ever desired and it seemed that just getting her into work of any kind was Mrs P's main objective. Coles didn't last, and nor did her next job working at the Film Development Company in the city which she started on 8 April. Nancy was sent out on a message and did not return. Instead she went first to the office of the Aboriginal Welfare Board and then to the Child Welfare Department to inform them of what she had done. She told them she didn't like the work, 'even though the conditions were satisfactory'.

On this visit to the Child Welfare Department, Nancy again asked for information about her mother. The file note states: 'Ward asked advice of her parentage and whereabouts of mother. Advised as disclosed by file' (CWD file note, 8 April 1947). It is not clear which file note Nancy was given – the one that gave her mother's last address or the one that said she was deceased. The subsequent report makes clear the dilemmas confronting both Nancy and Mrs P:

CWD Report, 11 April 1947

Nancy has a very awkward manner, is gauche in all her movements, abrupt in her speech, and gives the impression of being very rude and insolent – brought about mainly by her peculiar temperament, feeling of inferiority, and excessive sensitiveness about her colour ...

I met the girl on Strathfield Station the following morning ... Mrs P was with her. She was very loth [sic] to have the girl back, as Nancy had told her when she left her position on the Tuesday, that she intended to run away altogether. Mrs P felt that the worry and responsibility of not knowing when Nancy would return was too much for her. She said the girl was good in the home but entirely uncommunicative – she felt she was not happy and was full of resentment. Nancy denied this, stating she was very happy with Mrs P and wished to return to her. After a good deal of abuse on both sides, Mrs P agreed to give the girl another chance.

Nancy was still living with Mrs P and the Department recommended (18 April 1947) that she be classified as an 'adopted boarder'. The next job organised for Nancy was as a messenger girl for Garraway Heliographers but this didn't last either.

Things seemed to be spiralling out of control. It got to the stage that Nancy did not return at night either. She was seen each day but no one knew where she was sleeping. Nancy sais later that she had been visiting the 'Manpower' office (equivalent of Centrelink) where one of the officers was very kind and took time with her. He suggested Nancy join the Land Army, but she wasn't old enough.

Barely a month later, on 15 May, Mrs P asked for a Department Inspector to call because she was increasingly worried that Nancy went off every day without telling her where she was going and did not turn up at any of the jobs arranged for her. The next day Nancy went 'missing'.

CWD report, 16 May 1947

> I feel that this girl is incapable of holding a position. She is quite irrational in her behaviour and can be extremely dangerous. Under the circumstances, it would appear that if the girl does not present herself in the next two or three days that a warrant will have be taken out for her.

This is the first mention that Nancy was 'dangerous' but there is no evidence whatsoever in her file to support this claim. Also on 16 May 1947 an 'urgent' Departmental Report noted that Nancy had called in at Burwood Police Station to ask for money to get the fare to the city.

CWD report, 19 May 1947

> Mrs P rang me on Sunday morning 18/5 to report that she had seen Nancy in the choir at St Thomas' Enfield that morning. She asks that action be taken to locate the girl as she, Mrs P, is afraid of Nancy who, she says, is liable to resist and attack her.

Nancy loved singing and says that she had been determined to keep going to the choir. She said that she never attacked Mrs P physically, although she probably did give her verbal abuse.

Nancy was eventually taken into custody and appeared at the Metropolitan Remand Centre where she was remanded until 3 June 1947 so as to arrange for a clinical report. The tests were conducted by the Child Guidance Clinic and their report included the following comments:

Another story ...

Child Guidance Clinic, 4 June 1947

Intelligence: A Stanford Binet test (29.9.45) showed that she was intellectually advanced by two years, with an I.Q. of 116. The psychologist on that occasion found her emotional and overexcitable, alternately laughing and tearful. ...

Psychiatric: Nancy, who is attractive despite her obvious racial characteristics, came into the interview with initial resentment which might readily have developed into hostility. However, she responded to good humour, and talked freely and in a controlled manner. One feels that there is only a slight margin of safety between this mood, and a capacity to overreact emotionally to any circumstances which might stimulate a grievance ... [part of report missing] ... behaviour with a frequency which is somewhat disquieting, but which might be interpreted as protests associated with her inability to take a normal place in a white community, together with her uncertainty about her parentage. Conflict in this direction is thus expressed actively in the form of threats and outbursts.

This emotional energy will continue to be expressed in unacceptable methods, unless it can be directed into channels where she can find satisfaction and achievement, it seems wise therefore to test her at this stage in a vocation of her own choosing as a last challenge to her capacity to become stabilized. She may find nursing with a religious flavour, and with a purpose in keeping her expressed desire, a means of externalising her energies at present disorganized and unsatisfied.

I have discussed with Miss Inspector S, the possibility of placing her in a living-in job, as a wards maid, in a hospital where her duties might have a pseudo-nursing quality. Balmain Hospital accepts girls as probationer nurses at the age of 16 years; her advanced physique and intelligence should make her acceptable. Since her choice lies in the care of children, she may alternatively find work in a babies' home, the intervening nine months being regarded as a testing period to determine if she be sufficiently reliable temperamentally to succeed in the profession, upon which she cannot embark seriously until 18 years of age. ... If she fails in this instance, one would be obliged to admit that Nancy does not possess sufficient stability of purpose to succeed. [The letter continues but the remainder is unavailable].

When Nancy appeared before the Court again on 5 June, it was decided that she should not be returned to an institution, at least until she had been tried in work of her own choice – in a hospital. The Department arranged for her to start at Normanhurst Private Hospital in Ashfield where she would live in. She was placed on remand for six months on condition she attended work. Keeping tabs on Nancy was proving impossible. By 13 June it was recommended that a warrant be issued as Nancy had been out every night, wasn't conforming to the conditions of her remand and had stolen 10 shillings from a staff member. The matron reported, 'I'm afraid this girl is hopeless. She has lied consistently since she has been in the position. She has been out every night.' Nancy recalled a night at the movies with the cook and that, when she did run away, she took only the money she was owed by the matron.

She turned up at Bidura from where she was sent to the Shelter. On 19 June she was before the court again, facing complaints that she had also been 'very troublesome' during her week in the Shelter. The Magistrate remanded her and asked for urgent enquiries to be made at the Aborigines Welfare Board to see if she might be admitted to one of their homes, such as Cootamundra.

However, Nancy was once again committed to an Institution 'on a charge of being neglected, exposed to moral danger'. She was back in Parramatta, partly because that's where she said she wanted to be. At this stage Nancy claims she couldn't have cared less. She had given up hope.

While Nancy was in the Shelter, her case was discussed with Mrs E, an Aborigines Welfare Board Officer:

CWD report, 19 June 1947

Mrs E said that the girl could not be placed in an APB home. The only home for abo. girls is at Cootamundra but this home is only for orphaned and destitute girls under the age of 15. Delinquent or 'problem' girls like Nancy are not catered for. Mrs E stated that Nancy was in the Cootamundra Home from Dec '44 to Feb '45. her behaviour proved unsatisfactory and she was placed on the Abo. station at Moonacullah via Deniliquin for a trial. She was given sympathetic treatment on this station but the placement also proved a failure after 5 months.

Nancy found herself again subjected to medical examinations, which again found her intelligent – amongst other things.

CWD Report, 30 June 1947

Medical Certificate:

I hereby certify that I have this day medically examined Nancy Edwards, aet.15, and find that she is now of good physique, well nourished, has a carious tooth, is emotionally unstable, fairly bright mentally, and may have some moral sense.

The Child Welfare Department seemed at a loss to know what to do next and even approached Mrs P themselves this time to see if she could help them. It also realised that renewed efforts into finding Nancy's parents might help the girl – clearly by now this was a major preoccupation for Nancy.

CWD report, 13 August 1947

Although it was felt quite certain Mrs P would have nothing to do with this girl, a visit was made to her this week. She is definitely not prepared to do anything for Nancy, not even to the extent of writing or visiting her. This girl is worrying about her own mother – Ruby Josephine Edwards – unknown whether married or not – and begs couldn't an effort be made to trace her. Various contacts were made last time the girl was at Parramatta, but all came to nothing. The girl now asks could the Registrar General be approached, in the hope that some information might be obtained. The Aborigines Welfare Board informed the girl, when she was out, that they had located an uncle, or heard that there was an uncle living at Beaudesert, via Stony Gully, Mr Jack Edwards, who might have some information, or might be able to help her.

Recommendation: If possible that some contact be made with the Registrar General's office in an effort to trace this girl's mother.

An additional file note adds: 'It is strongly advisable that every reasonable endeavour be made to trace this girl's relatives, especially her mother. This branch will cooperate.' The Department then wrote to Jack Edwards of Beaudesert, apparently an uncle, on 19 August, to a Mrs Rutherford of Dalgety and again to the Aborigines Welfare Board on 20 August. How the Department had found information which linked Ruby to Jack Edwards or Mrs Rutherford is unknown but, in any case, this led nowhere. On 29 August the Board informed the Department that they had been unable to trace Ruby Edwards. The Department's search for Ruby included enquiries as far afield as Beaudesert, Dalgety, Delegate, Goulburn, Orbost, Bairnsdale, Nowra, Port Kembla and Redfern. It involved the AWB, the CWD, the NSW and Victorian police and resulted in a series of police reports. There is no other evidence of how this search was made. However, as the Edwards family were a large family in western New South Wales, it seems curious that enquiries among Aboriginal stations and reserves would not have located them. By then, of course, Ruby was better known by her married name but she had many kin who would have known her maiden name.

It seems Nancy herself was trying to repair her relationship with Mrs P at this time. By January 1948 she was upset because Mrs P had not acknowledged any of her letters.

CWD Report, 30 January 1948

Nancy mentioned that she had written a number of letters to her ex-guardian, Mrs P, and had not received a reply or visits and she seems to be very disturbed and worried by this. Mr Simms in discussing this matter said that Mr P had been to see Nancy with Mrs P while Nancy was in the Institution previously but on this occasion had phoned once and nothing else had been heard from the P family.

I visited Mrs P on 19.1.48 and she was most emphatic that she was no longer interested in Nancy as she was afraid of the girl whom she thinks is mental. She recounted Nancy's misdeeds right back to when Nancy had first gone into her home at the age of 8. Most of these were childish pranks which should have been forgotten long ago. She also said that Nancy had caught her [daughter] by the throat and the child still had nightmares about it, but as [the daughter] has written to Nancy saying she was writing unknown to her mother there does not seem to be anything in what Mrs P says. Mrs P says she is concerned with the upbringing of her own two children and cannot write to Nancy because if she does Nancy will later want to go into the home again either as a visitor or as a resident.

In discussing this matter with Nancy, it was obvious that Nancy feels the need of an older woman friend, whom she can regard as a mother substitute, and I do not think her regard for Mrs P is genuine other than that the woman is the only person she really knows well enough for her to idealise. Mr Simms mentioned a former guardian of Nancy's, (Mrs A) who works in Parramatta and called to see Nancy once, and is encouraging Nancy to write to her and visit her at the Baby Health Centre, Parramatta when out on shopping excursions. This should help Nancy break her attachment to the P [family] who do not want her.

This was an insightful report which identified some of the difficulties that Nancy had experienced and which had proved so unsettling for her. One can only wonder why there had not been reports of this nature produced in the past. From the Department's perspective, then, it was unfortunate that Mrs P changed her mind and got in touch with Nancy in March. All this did was re-establish Mrs P's erratic to-and-fro relationship.

CWD Report, 12 March 1948

The attached letters from the Police Department regarding the whereabouts of Nancy's relatives, have been discussed with Nancy, and she is disappointed that there is still no news regarding her mother.

Unfortunately her one time guardian, Mrs P has written again to Nancy and there is the same old conflict to contend with all over again. Nancy

Another story ...

at present is over confident that Mrs P has forgiven and forgotten, and that they are the best of friends again and that Mrs P will allow her to become a member of the family once more. Having seen Mrs P a couple of months ago when she was so decisive that she never wished to see or hear anything about Nancy again, I am rather at a loss to know why she bothered to write the short note she did, as it unsettles the girl very much. The letter was very brief and contained no news at all, Nancy replied with an eight page letter and is now impatiently awaiting further news.

Clearly by this time Nancy's skin colour was impacting a lot more on the way in which she saw herself. In the world of mid 1950s Australia she was being expected to enter, to have 'a bit of colour' was a real impediment. The Child Welfare Department seems to have given little thought to how to deal with this – either in assisting Nancy herself or in selecting employers. It is remarkable that they found Nancy's attitude 'unusual'.

However, in recommending Nancy's discharge from Parramatta in May, the Director did indicate that he was aware Nancy's skin colour might prove 'awkward' for her.

Letter, Superintendent of Parramatta Girls Home to Director, CWD, 22 April 1948

This girl has been one of our most interesting and difficult inmates. She has a marked infusion of Aboriginal blood and has for years shown unusual sensitiveness in this matter.

She is a recidivist. Much has been done for her by the Aborigines Welfare Board and this Department. She has been tried by many guardians. A great deal of patience has been exercised by many people in an attempt to help this girl. She was returned to this institution on the 19.6.47.

She had been with Mrs P when she was discharged on 10.3.47. She gave Mrs P so much trouble that that woman will now have nothing more to do with Nancy.

At the present time Nancy has maintained an improvement over a period of months. There seems little to be gained by detaining her still further at this Institution. Indeed, it may have an adverse effect upon her if this is done.

It is understood that District Officer Miss Doran has a prospect of placing Nancy in work in a private hospital. Nancy professes to have a desire to be trained as a nurse and this position, if approved for Nancy would give her the opportunity to discover whether her wish to become a nurse is real in fact. The position will become available in four to six weeks time.

One life, two stories

Nancy was discharged into the care of Mrs S, with whom she would board while commencing work at Sunbury Private Hospital in Ashfield. Mrs S had 'been attending GTS Parramatta for a number of years, giving the girls bible instruction on Sundays, therefore she is well known to CWD Officers connected with that Institution.' She moved to Mrs S's house on 27 June but on 20 July Mrs S urgently contacted the Department because 'Nancy is causing some trouble'. Nancy was taken into custody on 22 July and again charged with being 'uncontrollable'. Remanded for two weeks, the Court then decided to try her in country employment.

This remedy proved even worse for Nancy. On 12 August 1948 she was sent to work as a domestic at a property in Cobbadah. She lasted 24 hours. On her departure, she left a note for her new employer:

Nancy to Mrs C, 13 August 1948

Dear Mrs C

I am so sorry to do this but I miss Sydney too much I would not have known what to say to you that is why I am going like this. Mr Kelly will most probably get the rest of my things. I aim to walk to Barraba. I want to get back to the kids. It's too lonely here for me.

Thanking you for your kindness.

Yours sincerely,

Nancy

Nancy set off for the police station at Tamworth where she made the following statement:

Nancy Edwards, 15 August 1948, Tamworth Police Station

I did not like being at Cobbadah and it was too lonely. I arrived there on Friday afternoon, 13th August 1948, and absconded on Saturday 14 August at 4 pm and went to Barraba. I stayed with an officer of the Salvation Army until about 11.30 pm when I left and hitchhiked to Tamworth and came to the police station.

When I left Mrs Crowley's place at Cobbadah, I took a clock and torch belonging to her but I gave them back to her when she called at the Salvation Army Home last night. I have no complaint to make regarding my treatment by Mrs Crowley but the place was too lonely. I want to go back to Sydney. I miss the girls.

This last comment explains a lot of Nancy's behaviour. The girls she missed are those in Parramatta Girls Home. They were the only friends she had in the world. Much of Nancy's apparently bizarre behaviour can be

Another story ...

understood as a means of getting herself sent back to Parramatta. By this time, this was acknowledged by the Department but they had no desire to encourage her institutionalisation.

Nancy ended up back in the Metropolitan Girls' Shelter in Glebe on 17 August where she was remanded to appear in the Metropolitan Children's Court on 20 August.

Metropolitan Children's Court, 20 August 1948, Court Report

Bench: What was the trouble at Tamworth, Nancy?

Nancy: It was too lonely.

CWD Report, 20 August 1948

This girl appeared at MCC today. She was most anxious to return to GTS Parramatta where she has been for so long. Her reason being that she was happy with the girls there. I felt that if she were to return there she would be even more difficult to settle in the community than she is at present as she has become institutionalised. Therefore I have arranged that she be given a further opportunity of employment.

But Nancy proved as stubborn as the Department.

On Friday arrangements were made for her to be placed at a Convalescent Hospital in Mosman. Nancy went on Saturday morning and left on Sunday morning, returning to the Metropolitan Girls' Shelter.

Children's Court, Sydney, 23 August 1948

Bench: Is there anything you want to say, Nancy?

Girl: I don't want to go out again. I want to go back to Parramatta.

Nancy was charged, this time in the Children's Court, Croydon, as 'an uncontrollable young person within the meaning of the Child Welfare Act, 1939' and committed to Parramatta. The Department reported to the Court that: 'The girl won't be placed outside an institution set-up apparently' but they again record that Nancy asked to be sent back to Parramatta.

However, although Nancy was recommitted to Parramatta, before going she absconded from the Shelter with two other girls. All three were returned to the Shelter, charged as 'uncontrollable' and committed to Parramatta again in September 1948.

Things got worse before they got better. At 8 pm on 24 February 1949, having stayed out of trouble for some months, Nancy absconded with

One life, two stories

another girl. They squeezed through the window of the Cookery Room and out into the Hospital Block grounds. The police were notified and a warrant issued for them.

On 28 February the police found Nancy on a train.

Police report, 28 February 1949

Stated she had come from Singleton. Also stated that she had no ticket but that she had a number (26) on her back ... Taken off train at Hamilton ... Admitted having absconded from Parramatta.

Twenty six was the number by which Nancy was known at Parramatta.

Nancy's statement to police, 28 February 1949

[Written by Nancy herself] On Thursday night I left my class and went to Betty's class and I asked her to abscond with me. We went around and climbed over the Special Cooking. I had left a window open that afternoon. We opened the window. I climbed in and passed the tables out to Betty. We then stacked them up against the wall and climbed over out of the school.

Signed Nancy May Edwards

Witnessed by Constable X, 1st Class, Newcastle

Another story ...

On 2 March, Nancy appeared in the Newcastle Children's Court charged with 'travel on train without payment of fare'. Returned to Sydney, she appeared on 4 March at the Metropolitan Children's Court with her friend Betty to face charges of absconding, and break/enter/steal. They were clearly very rebellious by now and Nancy was seen as the influential ringleader.

The latter charge related to the fact that the two girls had broken into Bankstown Home Science School, had stolen clothing, cooked themselves a meal and stolen bikes. They were returned to Parramatta and given 48 hours isolated detention.

Court Officer's report, 4 March 1949

The Shelter advised: These [two girls] were troublesome at the Shelter. Necessary to separate them from the others. Quarrelled with the girls – one girl was crying and said Nancy stuck a needle in her. The girls made a bid to abscond – tried to get the stool to the wall. They refused to get dressed in their own clothes for court – would not tell the officer where the clothes were – so they are coming to Court in old Shelter clothes. Refused to have medical examination. Threatened to be troublesome coming to court – Police escort necessary.

But Nancy wasn't going to 'settle' at Parramatta either. She had learned a few things about how the system worked. She and three other girls 'attempted suicide'. Nancy knew this would get them a stay in the comfortable Reception House, where the staff were kind and the facilities good. She was right. On 5 March 1949 the four girls were sent to the Reception House in Darlinghurst where they would undergo psychiatric testing.

CWD Report, 11 March 1949

Attempt by four girls at the Training School for Girls, Parramatta, to commit suicide. ... No explanation can be offered as to why the incident occurred, but all the girls have unsatisfactory histories and are mostly unstable. On the advice of the Doctor, they were taken to the Reception House and have been certified as insane.

Parramatta ISG report, 11 March 1949

The Superintendent reported that on the night of 5.3.49 her conduct was such as to cause anxiety as to her sanity, and she was transferred to the Reception House on the same night. Nancy was examined by Doctors S and R, was certified as insane and was transferred to the Mental Hospital, Callan Park on 10.3.49.

So Nancy celebrated her seventeenth birthday by being admitted to Callan Park Mental Hospital. Was she insane? Shakespeare might have commented, had he known Nancy, 'If 'tis madness there be method in't'. Probably this report simply confirmed what some officials had thought all along. From their perspective it was a simple, uncomplicated way to understand this 'unstable' girl, a way that absolved them of the continued responsibility for her.

It is noteworthy that the Department, who has had care of Nancy since she was one year old, can call her history 'unsatisfactory' without reflecting on its own duty of 'parental' care and its own contribution to the making of this history. It is clear from reports that they felt they were doing a lot for her. However, a closer reading suggests that by continuing to find her one home after another, and interpreting any difficulties that arose as due to Nancy's personality, the Child Welfare Department felt they had adequately discharged their duty of care. Only in the case of Mrs P, and then only after a great deal of direct contact on the part of the Department, was a question raised about what Nancy had to deal with because of the instability of a foster parent. In all other cases, it is assumed that Nancy received good, stable, caring parenting. The files always imply that Nancy was moved due to faults of her own.

Callan Park report, 18 August 1949

Spent a day with Mrs P to explore possibilities for future employment. Desires to sit for the Nurses' Entrance Examination with a view to following that type of occupation. In the meantime she is prepared to accept a live-in domestic position if this can found for her.

Being in Callan Park didn't cure Nancy of her restlessness or her desire to find her mother. On 19 July she absconded from Callan Park and set off to see a friend from Parramatta, also called Ruby like her mother. Ruby was staying with a family in Wahroonga. It was a short excursion – Nancy was apprehended at Wahroonga Station and returned to Callan Park.

The relationship with Mrs P continued and Mrs P visited from time to time. The issue now confronting Nancy was what to do with herself when she became old enough to leave the care of the Department – which would be on her next birthday when she turned eighteen.

Nancy herself took an interest in what would happen next and often revisited her desire to do nursing. She met with the Director of the Child

Another story ...

Welfare Department in mid-August to discuss her future but didn't hear back from him.

Nancy writes to CWD from Female Ward 6, Callan Park, Rozelle, 6 September 1949

Dear Sir,

It is close on three weeks since my interview with you. I am really anxious to go to a position, but I suppose it is a bit difficult to find a person who would be willing to employ a person who has been in Callan Park, as well as a reformatory. Of course there could be other reasons but I am anxious to go to a position and study so that I shall be able to sit for the Nurse Entrance Exam. [rest of letter not available]

This letter received no response either and the staff at Callan Park must have been concerned for her too as they advised her to write again.
Nancy wrote a third time:

Letter from Nancy to Director CWD from Callan Park, 13 September 1949

Dear Sir,

I am sorry to be such a bother, but I have been advised to write to you again this week. I know you must think I am impatient but I think anyone in my case would be a bit queer that wasn't. Do you think I am not sincere about wanting to study nursing.

The Child Welfare, I understand, is my legal guardian until next year, so I really think you are the ones I should turn to. I think you mentioned that you are my friends. Have you forgotten that I exist or is it that you gave me so many chances before you just can't be bothered with me ... [lines missing] ... to interview me, but you never seem to come around the corner. Disappointments are terrible especially when you have them every day. If you cry with disappointment here you're told you are depressed and not well enough to go home. Please sir, I don't think it would hurt you very much to try and fulfill your promise you made to me, or have you forgotten that. Six months isn't very much time to brush up on every thing, if I really want to do it like I have told you then I must know everything off by heart without a mistake. Please sir, I am asking you to just give me one more chance ... [lines missing]

Eventually, on 21 September, she received a reply from the officer explaining he had been on leave. In his subsequent report it is clear he didn't have much confidence in Nancy. It also seemed that some of the communication between staff at Callan Park left something to be desired and that the treatment of Nancy was not always consistent.

CWD Report regarding Nancy's progress at Callan Park, 28 September 1949

She was placed in the Refractory Ward but the doctors interviewed could not ascertain why. Nancy said it was because one of the doctors 'did not like her and was anxious to make things unpleasant for her.' 'Dr K seems to think that Nancy had been placed in the Refractory Ward for giving insolence to one of the nurses in Ward 6. He was not sure of the details, etc but said that, although the girl was hard to manage, and not to be trusted, eg absconding on one occasion, she should be given an opportunity to prove herself outside. He said he did not suppose she would stay in her job but that there were a lot of people like that and that was not sufficient to keep a girl shut up'.

At least the doctor mentioned in this report was prepared to give Nancy a go. What is more amazing, given the detail in Nancy's file about her above average intelligence, was the report of Callan Park's Superintendent a couple of weeks later:

Letter from Superintendent, Callan Park to CWD, 10 October 1949

I have to advise that the above mentioned patient has recovered sufficiently to be given a trial out of hospital, although owing to her limited mental development it is felt that she will not adjust herself very well. If your Department is willing to take charge of the patient, I will discharge her.

Perhaps by 'limited mental development' he was referring to undeveloped social skills. It is curious, though, how little reference there is in Nancy's whole file to her educational abilities – or concern for their development. The expectation seems to be that, after a lifetime in their care, Nancy could not expect to do any work except domestic duties. But the Department did recognise the problem with the Superintendent's assessment.

But some Department officials had clearly given up – even on domestic work.

And just three days later, another report stated:

CWD Report, 14 October 1949, noting report from Callan Park

Despite this recommendation I still feel that this would only be feasible if Nancy had people of her own to whom she could go for protection. As it is, it would be

Another story ...

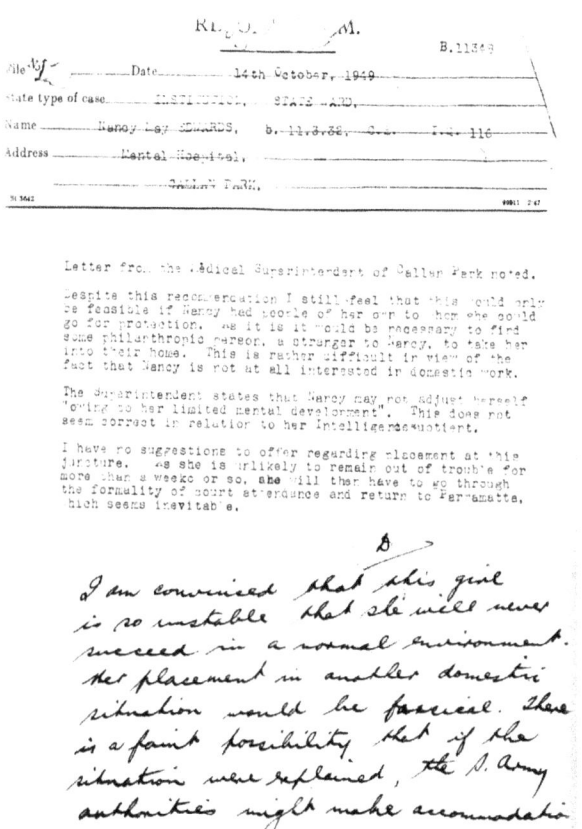

necessary to find some philanthropic person, a stranger to Nancy, to take her into their home. This is rather difficult in view of the fact that Nancy is not at all interested in domestic work.

The Superintendent states that Nancy may not adjust herself 'owing to her limited mental development'. This does not seem correct in relation to her intelligence quotient.

One life, two stories

CWD Report, 17 October 1949

I am convinced that this girl is so unstable that she will never succeed in a normal environment. Her placement in another domestic situation would be farcical. There is a faint possibility that if the situation were explained, the Salvation Army authorities might make accommodation available for Nancy at one of their hostels, to enable her to go to a factory job.

Despite the apparent lack of evidence for a serious enough mental or other disturbance to have put Nancy in the Refractory Ward, she is still there nearly two months later and this proves an impediment to plans that can be made for her. There is no record on file that the Department sought to discover the reasons for her allocation to this ward but on 18 November they filed a report stating that, while she was in this ward, she was 'obviously unsuitable for placement'. They took no further action at the time.

CWD report, 24 February 1950

At the Mental Hospital, Nancy's progress has been pleasing. Doctor M of the Hospital medical staff has advised that over the past four months, her conduct has been exemplary and he considers that Nancy has earned the opportunity to be placed out in the normal community once more. While it is doubtful whether her response to normal living will be satisfactory, Dr M considers she should be given this opportunity to effect her rehabilitation.

Nancy, on the other hand, seems to have responded positively to her impending release from Callan Park – which would coincide with her release from the care of the Child Welfare Department as well.

Nancy was discharged from Callan Park and transferred to Bloomfield Mental Hospital in Orange.

Eight days later, Nancy turned eighteen and the records stop. Nancy was now no longer the responsibility of the Child Welfare Department or a ward of the state. From this point on she had no further contact with state institutions. Despite the repeated predictions in her records that she would be unable to survive outside the framework of an institution, she did indeed survive. Not without her ups and downs, but these were of a different order and show that Nancy very quickly took responsibility for her own life.

The rest of that story is for Nancy to tell.

Another story ...

Timeline of Nancy's childhood years, 1932–50

1932, March	Nancy born in Sydney, in care of her mother
1933	Foster home 1: Merrylands, 5 yrs
1938	Foster home 2: Marrickville
1939	Foster home 3: Arncliffe, 6 mths
1939	Foster home 4: Willoughby
1940	Foster home 5: Bankstown, 8 mths
1940	Foster home 6: Strathfield
1944, April	Institution 1: Mulgoa, Penrith
1944, May	Foster home 7: Eastwood
1944, Dec	Institution 2: Cootamundra Girls' Home
1945, Feb	Foster home 8: Moonacullah Aboriginal Station
1945	Returned to Foster home 6: Strathfield Work trials
1945	Institution 3: Dalmar Childrens' Home, Carlingford
1945, October	Institution 4: Parramatta Girls Home
1947, March	Returned to Foster home 6: Strathfield
1948	Returned to Parramatta Girls Home (Institution 4) Work trials
1949, March	Institution 5: Callan Park
1950	Institution 6: Bloomfield
1950, March	Removed from care of CWD at 18 yrs of age

One of Nancy's favourite photos with the 'I've been everywhere' foot someone found for her on a day out. Photo by Mervyn Bishop (2001).

Reflections on living with difference

You have just read two stories. One is Nancy's own story, the story of a lived life. The other is Nancy's story told through an official, bureaucratic lens. The difference demands our attention. So much history, so many 'facts', are derived from written records which purport to be glimpses into lived lives. This juxtaposition of stories illustrates the limitations, even the distortions, within the written record. It shows how careful one must be in interpreting one without the other.

When Nancy first read through her own file she was shattered to learn how she had been viewed. She recalls her anger, hurt and bewilderment at the accusations, the labels, the silences and the distortions. But as she wrestled with how to deal with the way her story had been interpreted by the Child Welfare system of the time, she could also start to understand how the system within which she had been living made its decisions and how it impacted on her own life and the lives of other children. She could take the pressure off herself and her mother as she saw how both of them had been caught up in social and legal processes way beyond their knowledge or control.

The Aboriginal people who wish to tell their stories of removal, those involved in the Inquiry and its associated activities or who now write their stories, all face the problem of the power of written record. It is a dilemma that has now played out – disastrously – in the courtroom. People who draw on written records, interpreting official records as 'fact', relying on statistical data as 'evidence' claim a greater access to the 'truth', in this case, the truth of removal. They claim greater access to this truth than those people who lived their lives under scrutiny.

It is not that there is 'a truth'. It is not a case of choosing one story or another. But to choose an official record over a person's own testimony is to deny them their experience of what it has meant, for them, to be a human being, to be a person growing up, struggling with life's meanings, its ups and downs: a person with the right to claim meaning for themselves.

The meaning that was put by officials and foster parents on Nancy's experiences more often stemmed not from a knowledge of Nancy herself, but from stereotypes and convenient labels. It was easier to label her 'uncontrollable' than to explore with Nancy herself how her needs could be met within the families she was placed with. At times, it seems that her

Nancy talking to fellow University of Western Sydney students around the campfire, 1987. Photo: Gaynor Macdonald.

placements were not with people who wanted a child, a member of the family. Perhaps they wanted the kudos of fostering 'a poor Aboriginal waif'. Perhaps they found the money attractive. But it seems callous that a child should be removed because 'Mum' needed an operation, or sent to the Bidura 'depot' while 'Mum and Dad' went on holiday. One note on Nancy's file in December 1940, for instance, contained a request for the Department to care for Nancy while the family went on holidays:

> Guardian called and stated, "My husband will be going on holidays shortly for about three weeks. He will have an interstate pass. He cannot obtain a pass for Nancy. I would like the Department to mind Nancy while we are on holidays".

People do not normally give their children away to the Child Welfare Department under such circumstances.

Did Nancy mean anything to the people who looked after her? Yes, often she did. But they didn't seem to be able to adopt a sufficiently 'normalised' family relationship with her to make that work.

Difference

Nancy's story confronts us with the day to day reality of living with difference. In part, her story is one of her own capacity, and that of those she encountered through her life to recognise, understand and deal with difference. Her difference was not seen as an opportunity. It became crippling. Too Aboriginal to be accepted into white society, and not Aboriginal enough to be allowed to grow up with her own family or even with other Aboriginal people. Nancy's life was shaped by stereotypes rather than by her own capacities.

Finding out the official version of her history, while it increased Nancy's cynicism and anger in many respects, also strengthened her resolve to tell her own story. Aboriginal people have the unenviable task of educating non-Aboriginal people about their histories and their own particular forms of cultural expression. It is they who have had to take the initiative in response to a society that has been predominantly hostile. They have striven, and still do, for a space within that society in which to be what they are, what they have been and what they aspire to be. It is Aboriginal people who have been prepared to risk themselves to enable change.

Nancy took this risk in the hope that those who read her story would be prepared to bear witness to her experience of 'being Aboriginal' in Australia today. It was a courageous act. The life of a ward of the State has no privacy. Intimate details are filed away after a series of officials have had their say. The expectations of a ward are high. The child is not subject to the discretion of the wise parent, or the latitude given to those we love when they fall short of expectations, as we all do. Most of us take for granted the forgetting that takes place in valued relationships. The files of the Child

One life, two stories

Welfare Department and the Aborigines Welfare Board remember. They hang out most of the dirty linen and little of the clean. After all, it usually takes a 'problem' to have a notation on file. All the good days, the happy memories tend to go unmarked unless they have to be summoned to the cause of righting a wrong, as was the case when Mrs Q interceded for Nancy when she was sent to the Parramatta Girls Home. For Nancy there was no one to tell funny and endearing stories about her at her 21st birthday or when she married. The discriminatory practices and policies by which governments have sought to expel difference were written on her life, her emotions, her body. She lived daily with the conflict between unreconciled – sometimes irreconcilable – worlds of difference.

A space for difference

It is not sufficient that we just make a space 'over there' for difference – out on the missions, in institutions, on National Aborigines Day or Sorry Day, or spruced up and sanitised for the tourist industry. To live with difference, to respect it and explore its implications, requires that we hold on to an appreciation of our sameness, the interrelatedness of ourselves as human beings, the commonalities of our struggles, and the ways in which we are implicated in the struggles of others. Perhaps we can never fully understand another human being, but our very capacity to appreciate our diversity rests on the assertion that we are all equally human – and that our differences are the testimony to our creative capacities as human beings. Difference should not be read as separateness or as opposed to sameness. As Trin Min-ha (1989:79ff.) noted, difference is used by some as a tool to deny our capacity for shared communication.

Nancy, in her struggles as a child as much as in her political engagements as an adult, sought involvement, acceptance and recognition but in ways that protected and preserved her sense of self as distinctive, the fact of her difference and her right to be different. But it took her many years to learn how to celebrate and share that difference when everything around her strove to suppress it. It is, in fact, the creative capacity of people like Nancy to bring meaning to her own life and not succumb to the repressive policies under which she was raised that have forced Australia to address the moral and political issues of child removal in recent years.

Nancy, in the telling of her story and in her community involvements, such as helping in the building of an Aboriginal community in Liverpool in the south west of Sydney, in her speaking engagements and in Link Up, was committed to exploring the possibilities of 'reconciliation'.

Reconciliation means many things but whatever it means, it must start with recognition. The appeal to recognition is undervalued. It is important to any sense of identity and our identities, as Taylor (1991:45-46) puts it

Reflections on living with difference

'are formed in dialogue with others, in agreement or struggle with their recognition of us'. The relational dialogues through which Aboriginal people seek recognition – as in Nancy's case here – can be and often are extremely stressful. The public debates on the stolen generations illustrates this well.

The refusal of recognition can be very damaging to those denied it (Taylor 1991:49). The difficulty in Australia is that recognition of Aboriginal people means not only recognition of a shared humanity, equality, fairness and dignity – the recognition of human and civil rights – it also means recognition in terms of indigenous rights, including painful histories and, of course, difference.

It is European-Australian histories which have contributed to the way in which Australians see themselves, developing the images and metaphors that have served Australia to the present. Aboriginal histories, particularly in their interactions with Europeans, have been hidden. As is evident at the present time, bringing them to the surface involves a painful process of transformation and readjustment on the part of European-Australians themselves. It is far easier and more comfortable to recognise an 'Aboriginal traditionality' which has somehow miraculously survived and flowered than to recognise those Aboriginal societies and people who have remained distinct for the place they have had to hold in Australia's dark past.

The challenge for people who read stories such as Nancy's is that they will need to look at their own creations of selfhood and nationhood in order to understand the dilemmas which have to be faced in understanding how Aboriginal people have been designated as 'other' in Australia. The recognition of difference is a hard won right in Australia, a country with a particularly singular understanding of nationhood, which has not in the past legitimated difference and is still struggling with what it means in the context of multiculturalism. Even today the Anglo-Australian response to migrants is often 'why can't they be like us', 'if they come here they should be prepared to fit in and do it our way'.

Australia's mono-culturalism has a long history. There is early evidence in the dash across the continent to ensure the French did not 'settle' the west coast; in the gold fields which were unwillingly and violently shared with the Chinese; in the White Australia policy which contained migration; and, of course, in the segregation of Aboriginal peoples from the opportunities available to others in the mainstream of Australian life.

Australia has clung to a pedigree which required that difference be eliminated or assimilated. Difference has been defined as threatening the homogeneity of whiteness desired by the founding fathers of Australia's Constitution. Australia has long sought to protect itself from an assumed threat from Aboriginal people, from the 'Yellow Peril', from 'boat people' as it struggled to build a nation and national identity. Australia's mono-cultural identity has already been unsettled by non-Anglo migration. In Australia, for so long a nation which valued a mono-cultural way of life, difference has often been depicted as an impediment to social cohesion and harmony. Diversity has been valued only for its festive, exotic elements, contained in 'ethnic festivals,' in theatre, and in cultural products packaged for the tourist industry. But it has proved impossible to contain Aboriginality within such a comfort zone.

The threat to certain understandings of Australia as a nation that is posed by the Aboriginal presence makes it distinctive from other issues associated with multi-culturalism. The story of colonisation, of poisoned waterholes, of the missions and reserves, the Aboriginal Protection and Welfare Boards, civil rights campaigns, the Tent Embassy, stolen children, high rates of prison incarceration and deaths in custody, high illiteracy and unemployment, the fury over national land rights, and over the High Court's Mabo and Wik decisions – all these are chapters in the myriad histories of strategy and struggle designed to shape or exclude Aboriginal peoples in the making of 'nation', including the ways Australia tells its story of nation.

To come to terms with Aboriginal people, to be reconciled, is not just to add an identity – another culture in the multicultural mix. It is to shake the very foundations of nationalistic ideologies. National histories have to be rewritten, the images Australians have of themselves unsettled and recast. Aboriginal stories confront us with ourselves – and many people resist what they see.

Developing creative strategies

People draw on difference to reflect upon who they are and who they do and do not want to be. It is also a claim to distinctiveness as a cultural right and a necessary ingredient to cultural productivity, creativity and capacity to change. The creation of meanings and symbols associated with identity cannot be divorced from the political and economic realities within which identity struggles take place. How do people struggle? They look around for experiences, symbols and meanings that will help them deal with their immediate political tasks. They may look to their own past or to new ideas. But they don't look to readings they 'ought' to have of their prospective adulthood or an ideal of childhood. Nancy drew on whatever she could to make sense of her experiences.

Nancy's story is remarkable for the ways in which she developed strategies to see her through. People do not always act in ways others see as in their best interests – such interests can only be defined in a particular cultural, social and historical, as well as personal, context.

People everywhere, including, of course, children, have the capacity to bring meaning to their circumstances and afflictions. That is the remarkable capacity that we have as humans, irrespective of cultural differences. But each of us also starts with the resources that our own cultural worlds equip us with. Nancy was denied the opportunity to grow up in the world of her mother's people and did not find an alternative. Nancy's restlessness and search for meaning, translated as instability, increased with each decision to move her on to another 'home'. Carrying an enormous burden of loneliness which no one seems to have been able to bear witness to, she developed a determined resilience and independence, which translated as becoming uncontrollable. Sometimes expressed in her tenacity, sometimes in frustration and anger, sometimes in her wry humour, this could lead on an emotional roller-coaster not only for Nancy but for those around her – but those around her could choose not to live with its challenges and could move her on.

It is with some irony that one can later recognise that the characteristics of the 'uncontrollable' child were the very strengths that she drew on later in her life, to deal with a violent husband, the life-changing experience of going to university, of becoming involved in Link Up. It is such strengths which enabled Nancy, when confronted by ill-health and confined to a wheelchair or her 'red bus', to raise seven grandchildren and take on numerous speaking engagements.

How to be 'the good citizen'?

Nancy did not see herself as 'belonging' and clearly those who made decisions for her, even those most concerned for her, did not see her as belonging to their notions of an 'us' either. Nancy's loneliness stemmed in part from being caught between worlds, into neither of which was she adequately socialised or accepted. Nancy's dilemma, unbeknown to her when she was a child and a realisation that dawned only slowly, was that these two worlds did not accept or respect each other either. There was no room for meaning to be produced in the space between them.

Not just through removals but in many different contexts, all Aboriginal people have been part of a minority managed through specialised institutional structures, from Welfare Boards to ATSIC. The mode of incorporation of Aboriginal people throughout the twentieth century has been governmental. This has applied to individuals, such as Nancy, as well as to whole Aboriginal communities. Nancy, like so many others, was subjected to forms of governance designed to shape them into a particular kind of 'good citizen' – but not the 'normal' citizen expected of other members of the society. Rather, into a form of obedient servitude, into the lower status to which Aboriginal people were so often seen to belong. Why else would a child of above average intelligence be deemed capable only of housework? But nor could Nancy as 'good citizen' be allowed to become an 'Aboriginal citizen' – she was not different enough for that!

One life, two stories

The Australian state has managed Aboriginal difference by keeping it at a distance and developing strategies for its elimination or containment. People who were defined as 'part-Aboriginal', who were too fair, threatened the clear distinction between a white us and a black other. Nancy, as with so many of those who were removed, fell into this threatening space in between.

In recent decades there has been a political and legal space within which Australia's Indigenous peoples, Aboriginal people and Torres Strait Islanders, could challenge the racist structures of Australian society. But maintaining this space requires the rewriting of Australia's history, and a society prepared to learn to live with difference. The prerequisite which has proved too difficult for many is that Australians bear witness to Aboriginal experiences of being Australian. This demands not only that one bear witness to trauma. It also demands that one bear witness to difference: acknowledge it, allow it to flower, learn how to adjust to living within a world of difference that does not have to be suppressed, marginalised or institutionalised. This is easier said than done and there is a long way to go. Nancy was one of those people trying to develop a path.

While one cannot talk about Nancy's life outside of the total context within which Aboriginal people have been represented, treated and managed by the state over time, we must also take account of the specificities of her life, of the lives of others with similar but always distinctive stories of removal. These are children whose conditions were not of their choosing but who, within significant constraints of power and knowledge, tried to make sense of their lives. Nancy's story also demonstrates that the state is not monolithic, all pervasive or all powerful. Even in a situation in which she had little or no control, she managed to create meanings for herself which made sense – to her – of the constant moving, of the lack of the love she sought so constantly. Her own story, in contrast to the one on file, is a story of the ways in which she brought her personal resources into play at different times so as to address the ways in which she came to understand and attempted to deal with particular situations. But the rebelliousness and the wanderings which helped her – from her perspective – to hold on to the meanings she had developed for herself, so she could be strong, so she could cope, were not considered strengths but weaknesses in a society that demanded conformity and submission to a high degree.

When policy takes insufficient account of difference – whether of age or ethnicity or gender – it is not hard to see why certain situations give rise to unmanageable contradictions. In this case, these are left for a small child to sort out. Nancy seems quite early to have developed a sense of this and, as she says, to have become reflective and cynical at a much earlier age than is expected of children – at least happy and accepted children. Combining

Nancy's story with the written records, it is not difficult to see the problems which produced bewilderment, confusion and despair on the part of the child, foster parents and Department as 'control' of this child became more and more elusive.

Nancy's story is not the story of a motherless, powerless child. Rather, it is a remarkable story of a person struggling with what it means 'to be' when the conventional cultural and social resources available to children are not available. This is a struggle which so many removed children have had to go through. Lip service was paid to the need for the welfare of the child but, as Nancy experienced for herself, images of caring for an Aboriginal child were often restricted to a crude romanticism associated with unreflective missionising zeal. 'Care' meant showing off a pretty and exotically different small child. This romanticised view of childhood is devoid of humanness and of the enormity of commitment involved in bringing up children in complex worlds.

Children have tended to be invisible in our society, coming into their own as people, in their own right, and with rights, only in recent decades. In this invisibility they were underestimated. Aboriginal children were even more invisible. The importance of family was regarded differently if the family was Aboriginal. Did many Australians see Aboriginal people as having different feelings and emotions? Did they think they loved and cared less? How else could one account for the extent of removals 'for their own good', for bureaucratic 'welfare' decisions made in the cases of children in care which would not have been made for children in white families?

These were differences Nancy saw every time she was sent to Bidura and could compare the lives of non-Aboriginal children she encountered there. It is not unexpected, but it is sad and confronting, that Bidura – the revolving-door child-processing 'depot' – and Parramatta Girls Home were the two places where Nancy found special friends. Outside both Aboriginal and non-Aboriginal social worlds, these institutions provided liminal ('between') spaces in which these liminal girls encountered and re-encountered each other.

Nancy's life was one of conjuncture and disjuncture. Standard representations of the 'neglected child', the 'uncontrollable child', or the child who is 'better off' in institutional or foster care cannot grasp the contradictions, paradoxes and ambiguities of specific lives. These labels cannot show how a succession of foster families, staff of the Department of Child Welfare, the Aborigines Protection Board and other institutions, the police and the girls at numerous schools, all contributed to produce the imaginative strategies by which Nancy transformed herself – from homeless, lonely child, to rebellious and 'uncontrollable' adolescent, to an unsure adult, and eventually into the confident and articulate woman who spoke to the New South Wales Parliament in 1997.

One life, two stories

Was Nancy a 'stolen' child?

Was Nancy 'stolen'? The records are silent about how Nancy was taken from her mother. We cannot know the precise circumstances which led to this young mother having to part with her child, a child for whom she had already cared for over 14 months. Much later, a file note states she was signed into care but we should be careful of making assumptions about Nancy's mother's desires. She would, in any case, have had little say in an era in which Aboriginal people, women and young people had little say in controlling their circumstances – and Ruby was all three.

Nancy's first foster mother certainly believed Nancy's mother wanted to keep her. She told Nancy that her mother had been told she could claim Nancy back once she had a job. Ruby did return to Sydney for Nancy, having found a job in Ivanhoe – only to be told she could not take her daughter back and should go, as she was making a nuisance of herself. The authorities refused her access to her child. Nancy would not know this for many years. Even now she finds it painful to think of the impact that decision had for her mother as well as for herself.

Yes, Nancy was stolen because the severing of the relationship between mother and child, whether voluntary or not on the part of her mother, meant that Nancy and her mother were thereafter denied all knowledge of each other. Being made a ward of the Court did not imply that a person should be denied knowledge about and access to their parents and community. It did not give foster parents or the Child Welfare Department the right to later tell Nancy her parents were 'deceased'. Fostering was not intended to lead to the irrevocable severing of a natal bond – as was required of adoption at that time. Nancy was stolen – from her mother, her country, her roots, her sense of belonging, her right to grow up in an extended family and share in its cultural knowledge.

Life was pretty scary

After Bloomfield

Being in the institutions for so many years, where everything is laid down for you, you just have to comply. You don't have to make any decisions for yourself. To get out in the big wide world is a pretty scary thing. I didn't have a family. I didn't have friends. And I was angry, so my reactions to people were not the best. In fact I daresay I could have been called an objectionable person. It took me a long time to realise that there were some people that could be liked. That I could like some people. As for paying rent and things like that, I had to learn all that. I had to learn that if I had a few bob, I had to learn how to handle money. I had to learn how to buy food, I had to learn how to buy clothing, so I could look respectable. I had to learn to keep a roof over my head so I could be clean. Often I slept out. I was a homeless person. So it took me a long, long time to get to the stage of being what some people would call normal. When I look back on it now, it was a pretty scary time, and I probably didn't really adjust until I had Peter.

I met Pete's dad at Bloomfield. He was working there. I fell madly in love with him and thought, 'It's about time I got out.' I loved singing and they asked if I'd like to go down and join the musical society. We were doing the Desert Song. This white woman, she was playing the white sheila, and because I was dark they got me to play Azuri, the native girl. Then I found I could sing much better than most of them. It was just so wonderful.

We loved music, the pair of us. That was our passion. I remember once I was singing behind the curtain when we were having a performance, and he had to sing in the background to echo what I was singing. He came up behind me and he put his arms around me and he was singing these high notes. That's when my heart stopped. My heart was thumping so hard. Here I was experiencing love for the first time in my life, the very first time. It was just amazing.

One life, two stories

Nancy, 2003. Photo: Jane Mears.

He took me to a ball out at Fairbridge Farm one time. He had a little Sigma, you know, the little dicky seat type, and he'd driven me out there, and we drove over this puddle, and when I got out, there'd been a hole in the floor of it and the mud had come up and got all over my dress. I wasn't really pleased. I went inside and got it cleaned up pretty well. He did not like me dancing with anybody. And me, being the bitch I was, would get up and dance, and of course him being in the band, he couldn't come down. When I think about being young!

Then I found out I was pregnant. I said, 'I'm pregnant, I have to go to Sydney and get away from here. We have to lead our own lives.' Well of course, it was the best bloody thing that ever happened to me, having my son. I didn't go back on my word. I didn't. He was my true love. After I had Peter that turned my whole life around. I thought this little boy would give me unconditional love. I won't ever have to prove anything to this little boy. We'll just love each other and that will be it. And that's the way it's been. He still gives me unconditional love. The

most amazing thing was having a little son like this. A good friend.
That's how children should be.

Even though I loved his father desperately and would have done
anything for him, it was no incentive when you realised that the love
affair was not going to go anywhere. Once again, you really weren't
worthwhile. This is how I felt. But when I had Peter, I suddenly had
a whole change of outlook. I thought, I'm this little boy's mother,
this child depends on me, I love him desperately. I can't let anything
happen to me. I had to steel myself to do some things that really
weren't very pleasant for me, and were very difficult for me. I had to
learn to keep my big mouth shut and not say what I thought. I had
to learn, well, all the activities of everyday living and survival. As he
got older things became easier and I became more steady in working
towards my goal, which was to be a nurse. I began to get jobs that were
in hospitals. And finally, Pete and I made it.

Marriage

That's when I met Reinder. I'd already known him when I was a
younger person in Orange. He had these five little boys. It wasn't a
love match. It was me being noble, and thinking, 'If I marry him, we
can get all these kids together and we'll live happily ever after.'

But it was not to be. I loved the boys. They'd had a very hard life.
But he and I were not meant to be married. He was a very cruel man
and a very violent man. He was not only violent to me and Peter, he
was violent to his own children.

He'd come home with his pay, take out a few dollars and throw
it at me, 'That's your pay.' I said, 'Oh, thanks. Now where's me
housekeeping?' He didn't know what to think. 'Well, if it's my 'pay'
then my pay's going in my pocket. Now where's the housekeeping?'
He said, 'What do you spend all the money on?' I said, 'Come on,
come and help me get the shopping today.'

So he did. Off we went with the supermarket trolley. And he's
throwing in this and throwing in that. And I'm watching and not
saying a word, I'm thinking, beauty, beauty! This he'll have, and this
and this. When we get to the checkout it's all totalled up and he's got
his money ready, and I remember it came to about $104. In those

days that was a lot of money. When the girl says, 'That's $104, sir,' he nearly had a heart attack. But he paid it. No more questions regarding my shopping ability.

I remember him taking me to Henson Park and then having to pay for my ticket. I was putting up with this because I was pregnant at the time. He'd say, 'I wouldn't go and watch that game, what a stupid game, running up and down with a ball and then throwing it away.' I'd say, 'Yeah, just as bad as kicking in a way, I suppose,' meaning his soccer. Anyway, he goes and gets what he thought was my ticket, but the guy gives him two tickets with the change. He realised he'd bought two tickets but he was very gutless and he wouldn't say. So he had to come in and watch the game with me. Well, didn't he enjoy it! He was jumping around in his chair – but didn't say a word.

'Oh, I'm going to commit suicide,' he says one day. 'I'm going to take all these pills.' 'Hang about, babe,' I said to him. Then I put them all on the table. 'One for you and one for me, one for you and one for me.' 'You'd be a smart bitch.' 'Too bloody right,' I said. 'If you think you're going to leave me here with all the kids on my own you've got another thing coming.' Changed his mind then!

I had known him when we were young. I knew him when I was going with Peter's father. We were sort of all teenagers together, you know. I'd known his wife all that time. She'd run off – I didn't know why then. I'd known his boys since they were born and here they were, dumped by their mother. These little boys – it worried me so much that they'd been put in homes, so I married their father.

I thought getting married to him was the right thing to do, that putting up with his shit was the right thing to do. But that was only 'cos I felt sorry for the boys, his boys. I thought it was the right thing to do for those boys then and I still think it was. Because at least I sort of got them all together again. The eldest one who died, with cancer of the kidney, probably realised the most what I tried to do. He was the most like Peter and showed a lot of affection for me. He would stand by me, he was the one who seemed to understand. I kept in touch with them all. They were really nice boys. I still see some of them, like Brian. Our boys are named after them, Brian, David and Albert.

I suppose in some ways we were compatible. There were a lot of times we enjoyed each other's company. But I couldn't cop the drinking. I couldn't cop the abuse. I couldn't cop being told that I was nothing but a stupid black bitch. I thought I was doing the right thing by putting up with it because of the kids. When I finally left him and started getting on my own feet, I took them all with me until they found a place to all live together.

By the time I left him, I had Megan and David of course, his kids were old enough to go and do their own thing. As soon as they were old enough they got jobs and got on with their lives. I kept in touch with them all those years. It was only after the eldest boy died that I lost touch with them. I think that was sad for Megan and David.

I finally left him. It was the best thing I ever did with my life. Peter said to me in the end, 'If you go back to him, Mum, I will have to leave the house.' When I thought about it I thought, what am I doing? He was being violent to David, my baby. He was being violent to his boys, sticking forks into their faces and horrible things like that. Bashing them, bashing me. So I made the clear decision that I would leave him, and I took all the kids with me. We set up shop in Petersham, and the boys got their own flat in Summer Hill. I lived in Petersham and I worked at Summer Hill, so I still had a lot of contact with them. Peter helped me by looking after Megan and David while I went to work on night duty, and he went to school in the day time to Tempe Boys High. As I've said, I don't know what I would have done without him. Peter the rock. I couldn't have given him a better name.

Peter

My first born child, Peter, was the first thing I ever had in my life that belonged to me and I belonged to him. And we were a team right from the word go. I said to him, 'Oh well, we're starting out now together.' This was only a few hours after he was born and I'm talking to him like this, like he was 93 years old. And he's always loved me unconditionally. He's been good to me all his life and he's always been there for Megan and David. He used to get a bit cranky with Megan and David now and then but I think he was just being the big brother. But he helped me bring Megan and David up, minding them at night when I went to work and if I was working at the weekend. He's been my son, and he's also been my very best friend.

David

The next one was David. If ever you have seen a beautiful child it was David. He had fair hair, he's got light coloured eyes like me, and this innocent face. Such a handsome little boy. He was a very soft child. Peter loved having a brother. David was a bit of a loner, a bush boy. He'd feel the need to get out in the bush and off he'd go. But he always kept in touch. When I moved to Brewarrina he came out there too. He loved the bush. That's when he met Carmel, on one of his trips over to Bourke. They had a big family together. Now they've gone their separate ways, although they keep in touch for the kids' sake.

Megan

Then I had Megan, my first girl. It was so different having a girl. Because I had five stepsons too. So there were seven boys and here was a girl. It was so different. It was nice to be able to buy pretty things. We got on real well together until she got to be a teenager, and then we started fighting. First it started about the way she used to roll her socks down to go to school. I remember saying to her, don't roll your socks down. So, we had a few barneys, but once she had Peter Goodgebah, suddenly we were both mums. It makes a lot of difference in a girl's life to have her own children and realise, 'Hey, this is what Mum went through. This is what Mum put up with.'

She just got emotional when she saw my family tree for the first time in 2002. ' I do belong', she was saying. Yes, there is a wider family – but she'd never had that experience. Nor did I. Of course, now I have grandchildren – and that's been better but I had to create my family.

But even though they were all so different, they were all just as much loved as each other. They made my life very happy. 'Cos when you grow up with nobody and then you've got these kids, it's a big difference in your life.

Life was pretty scary

Nancy (2003) with her three children (clockwise): Megan (2001), David (2003) and Peter (2001). Photos: Gaynor Macdonald.

They said I wouldn't be good enough

Graduation Day 1988: Diploma of Applied Science (Nursing)
I wore my colours. And when I reached out to shake hands my colours showed.

The mob up the back made enough noise anyway. The Koori pride was shining through. And I really noticed the Koori pride when my friend, Jimmy Tyson, Biliyana, a real big guy, he was, he was that full of emotion. He said, 'Nance, I felt that proud when you went up there. I was nearly going to start yelling out "Land Rights".' I said, 'Well, I'm glad you didn't, I'm glad you didn't darling.' It really did something to me when he said that – it made me feel proud that he felt that way and that he wanted to call that out. It was a true Koori reaction to call out, but I'm glad he didn't. It was a very funny moment. God love him.

There was only one person in that whole University I could say that I felt animosity towards, only this one person. She was the only one and she was a horrible woman. I heard that she'd said, before my graduation, 'But what if she comes on in native dress?' Meaning, like, with me boobs bare. I would have loved to have done it to spite her. But I was really annoyed in one way that she thought I would do that to my peers – I mean, I had more respect for them. I loved all those kids that I went through with.

When I came up, Betty – Betty Anderson, Head of School – was standing there. She calls my name out and I come up. And you know how you have to bob to them and tip your hat? Well, I said to Betty, 'Please excuse me, Betty, if I don't bow to you, but I'm not bowing to any white person this year, 1988.' I just walked across and I nodded my head to her in respect. I bet Betty was thinking, 'What's she going to do when she gets to the Principal?'

But I just turned and walked across and I gave Judith a wink as I walked over. Then David – David Barr, Principal of Macarthur

Institute of Higher Education – spoke to me. He gave me a little talk and said nice things, like, 'You're a wonderful person' and all that sort of stuff. I liked David, and I liked Geoff Alcorn, Deputy Principal. Geoff was always very good.

Of course, afterwards there was a riot and we all went crazy and whooped and hollered and had photos taken and hugged and carried on.

Everybody knew that this was a unique moment, and yet we behaved as though it was no different to anything else. And that was an acceptance that meant it was special but we didn't have to do anything to make it special. It just was. That was really the culmination of everything. We had a lovely day. It really was a beautiful day. It really was terrific.

I finally got to university

I've wanted to be a nurse from when I was eight years old and so I worked in nursing homes looking after old people for 27 years. All those years my main concern was bringing up the kids on my own and seeing they had a good education. I think I had about three jobs in all that time. Eventually I'd get sick of the people nagging and whingeing and I'd go to another place, but all in the same area of nursing. I'd walk from one job to the next, really. I know that the matrons for whom I worked trusted me and were quite happy with my work and ability, my caring for the patients. I could always communicate with the patients.

Memories of that day from Judith Townsend, School of Nursing, Macarthur, April 2002

Graduation was hugely exciting. I've got some wonderful photos of Nance. It really was terrific. We were very proud of our two Koori students – Nance and Eunice. We'd really connected. All Nancy's Koori family were there. Just amazing.

And the roar that went up when Nancy was called up to the podium! Betty was beaming from ear to ear, we were all there. During the ceremony, interestingly, we played it straight down the middle. So while there was a huge roar for Nance and loud applause and we all smiled broadly and smiled at her and she looked at us, neither she nor her family nor anyone else did anything other than to fit into the absolute

They said I wouldn't be good enough

Nancy, able to relax after her graduation ceremony in May 1988, celebrating with fellow students, and the staff who were just as proud and delighted. Photo: Gaynor Macdonald.

normal academic mould at graduation. I think it was a better statement than anything else she could have done, to just be herself, to be proudly herself, but at the same time be just like everyone else. To not stand out from the crowd, to be just totally accepted into this community of scholars – that was the most powerful thing.

And to walk across without a stumble, without hesitation, to shake the Vice Chancellor's hand, shake David Barr's hand, receive her testamur and walk off with her head held high, just like everybody else. It was just the most wonderful thing.

I knew I should have been a registered nurse, deep in my heart I knew I was capable. But when the course at UWS Macarthur came up, I was talking to a friend of mine who mentioned it, I said, 'No, I wouldn't be good enough for that'. But she sent away for the papers for me to see. I'd thought about it before but I'd never done any sort of course in my life, just worked and raised the kids.

It was always the entry qualifications they wanted even in the hospitals for a nurse's aide and I knew I wouldn't be accepted. It was my friend who sent the application in. I could have hit her. I didn't even know. I got a letter, you know, sending me all these other forms to fill out. She thought she was being smart so I filled them out, sent them in – and got accepted! It was really great.

Well, I don't know why I thought I'd have any more of a chance this time. I just thought I'd have a go. I had the papers in front of me so I thought I'd just send them off. The fact that somebody else got the papers and put them in front of me made a big difference. This friend of mine had a very good job and she must have thought I had the ability. When the papers arrived, I knew who'd done it. But that made me think that someone believed I was capable. It gave me the push to go but I still didn't think I'd get in.

When the letter arrived to go for the entrance examination I got all excited. I was working on night duty and I had to go the University the next morning. When I got to the front door I thought, 'I can't go in here.' But I'd look a bit of an idiot turning round there and going back.

It was up near the library and I walked in and sat right up the back so I wouldn't be too conspicuous. I suppose I hoped that if I was really quiet they wouldn't notice I was Aboriginal. The staff supervising were really good and I felt a bit more comfortable. I thought, 'She's not too bad, she hasn't noticed.' Little did I know that she was Italian, one of an ethnic minority herself.

I sat down and I was so tired. My head was dropping and I thought, I really have to concentrate. When I looked at the paper I thought, hey, that's not really hard. Having nursed for 27 years the test covered things I knew a lot about.

Then I got the letter. We'd done the test in October and the letter arrived in January. In the meantime I thought they'd forgotten all about me. I didn't know it took so long for things to be processed. But the letter came. My kids were excited, but I still had doubts. Finally I thought, 'Yes, I'm going to have a go.'

But then enrolment nearly turned me off again. It was such a bunfight. I suppose it was all organised but a thousand others and I didn't know what we were doing and we were lined up for hours.

Finally I got there and put my name down and then paid the fees. That was a big worry but I managed to scrape it together. I don't know if I borrowed it or what, but I had it. If I'd known the Aboriginal Unit was there I would have gone to them and said, 'OK, now what do I do, where do I go and get some support?' Later I found out. The people were very patient and helpful, but I would have felt much more confident on the day if I'd known that bunch was there. They were nowhere in sight and I had to do it alone. But then, I hadn't told anyone I was Koori either.

I thought I had to remember it all, everything we were told on Orientation Day. I was trying to concentrate. Every time someone got up to speak I thought, 'How can I remember all this?' It was so emotional. I had a really terrible headache. I was terrified I'd fail on the first day. I was wondering, 'What am I doing here?' But I had to laugh when Judith Townsend said to the boys, 'And you don't wear coloured socks under your nursing uniforms!'

Then I saw this other Koori girl. I was looking at her and thought, 'We'll get together after this and have a talk', which we did. She was Eunice Gardiner. We both thought this other girl was a Koori too – until she opened her mouth. We said, 'Hi' and she said 'Hi' in that accent of hers, and we both said, 'Oh you're not Koori.' And she replied, 'No, what's that?' Eunice and I cracked up. This was Josie Lanaghan. She turned out to be Maltese, but there was a bond there between us, probably because we'd been through orientation and were feeling totally washed out and thought we'd probably not get any further than this. It was a terrible feeling, but then we started laughing. Kooris have a terrific sense of humour and to laugh about it made us feel more comfortable, knowing we'd made friends, the three of us and that on our first day we'd been there to help each other out. We had the same weird sense of humour. All through our years studying, the three of us worked as a team. We did all our tutorials together.

Once we had to make a film about interviewing a patient, with a mental health problem I think it was. I have never seen anything so funny in all my life. Josie was the interviewer and Eunice the interviewee. So Josie was trying show empathy and understanding. I'm doing the filming and I'm watching Eunice. She was trying to look like she was a patient. Every time Eunice would try and give an answer, Josie would go with the questioning. You could hear me, behind the camera, start giggling. Poor Eunice jumped up, we were nearly rolling on the floor, laughing. Every time Josie would ask a question, Eunice would cross her legs, very exaggerated. It was the body movements, it was a real comedy skit. I wish we had kept that film. It was the funniest thing. We did finally settle down and do it. And we didn't get such a bad mark for it. We wasted a lot of time laughing, though. We were a good team.

On the day I found my Mum, we had a tutorial on, and the two of them were terrified because I was going away. I said, 'I'll put my bit on a tape'. So I put it on a tape and went away. That night I phoned them up to find out how the tute had gone. They did better than if I'd been there. It was good fun.

At our first psychology class I thought, here's a go. Then the lecturer turned round and laughed at something. Everyone was sort of tensed up but she immediately put everyone at rest. She was marvellous, she got us talking about things and I was caught up. Nobody seemed the least concerned there were two Aboriginal women in this course. Mind you, there were women, and a few men, from all over. They came from Europe and South American countries to the Pacific Islands and outback NSW.

Early on there was frustration from never having written anything down. It's not something that's handed down to Kooris, we did everything orally and suddenly we had to do five pages on something. I knew what I wanted to say but I couldn't write it down, so assignments were always in the box with only minutes to spare.

We had a tutor in the Aboriginal Unit, Jane Perkiss, who would look at our work and provide feedback; she was a good guide. But we had a lot of work and if an Aboriginal person is doing something in non-Aboriginal society we have to prove ourselves ten times more than the non-Aboriginal people. I don't feel that so much nowadays, but at University it made me feel sick that I'd put in a lesser assignment than the girl over there who'd been right through high school. It really worried me that I'd be letting down my people by not being as good as that person.

Later on I just decided to be me, but that was the result of going through higher education. I became a completely different person. I not only graduated with a piece of paper to say that I'm a registered nurse and that I've done my course, but I graduated as a person. So it was good, it gave me self confidence, taught me not to be so aggressive with non-Aboriginal people and taught me to be assertive.

In the end I did very well, averaging about 70-75% on assignments. I enjoyed the problem-based Health Breakdown subject because it showed me a different way of putting things down which didn't require traditional scholastic ability. I did an Aboriginal Studies elective and that was terrific because we interacted with both Aboriginal and non-Aboriginal students and that helped.

I bought myself a thesaurus and dictionary and did a lot of reading to see how other authors wrote things. I hope they now tell Aboriginal students about such resources – half of them couldn't even say the words let alone use the books properly.

One of the problems is that many Kooris speak only Aboriginal English, but because they are Australian they are expected to speak English like everyone else and to express themselves in white [standard] English. Aboriginal English can be really different and it seems Aboriginal people get no recognition for that language problem, yet they can see other ethnic people being accepted with similar limitations. In other Faculties maybe they don't have quite the same problems because they've been teaching Aboriginal students much longer. In Nursing they were only just starting to come to grips with the needs of Aboriginal students, whether it was about English expression or traditions of behaviour.

But getting back to our problem-based approach in Health Breakdown. We were made to think it out, work it out and come up with some workable solution. When I look back, I loved that subject because of the freedom it gave us to deal with the situation in our own way. Our little Koori study group probably attacked the problems a totally different way from other people, but we came up with good results. It gives you freedom to use your own way of thinking. When classes were more structured I did it, but I probably struggled a bit more because then I was worried about the outcome and had to know exactly what the lecturer wanted.

I always found time a real problem. It was a very hard thing to come to terms with. I always thought if I had a little bit more time I could have done a better job. I always wanted to explore a bit more but there wasn't the time to do it, so you just put down what you thought you'd come up with. But there will always be time constraints and we have to come to terms with that.

To Aboriginal people time is different. Meal times are never set at a fixed time. We eat when we are hungry. The sun and the moon and the seasons guide us, not clocks and watches and deadlines. Deadlines and submission dates are hard to get used to. I was always under pressure. The limited time was a real problem, but there was no 'Koori time' here and that affected most Aboriginal students. But even with the time constraints, if there are no rigid structures within a course, like lectures and tutorials, or weekly tests we do better. With a learning package in a three or four week module I knew that at the end I had to do whatever I had to do, but I still had the freedom within those weeks to do what I liked with it, rather than this week do this and next week do that. But it's also a way of thinking about things and presenting them.

Sometimes I think Kooris would make good detectives. We like to inquire, enjoy solving a puzzle. But when it was presented in black and white I found it so boring. In the problem solving approach there are a range of issues which have to be covered. If I came across something interesting in the middle I could say, I don't have time to do that right now, I'll do the main work but I'll come back to that later. And I often did. I would go back and look at that issue to see if it was what I thought it was. You must have a main goal. If you see anything else that's interesting, well, it won't go away, you can go back to it later.

Clinicals I loved. They were really enjoyable, hands on, applying what we had pushed into our brains. I had good skills and when I got into the clinical it was great. But never once did we visit or work at any Aboriginal centres. We went to white preschools but we've also got black preschools in the city, but we never went there when I was going through. We didn't visit one Aboriginal health centre which would have been good because there are a lot of health problems which I found out about later and which I could have got some grounding through such placements. I also think it would have done the non-Aboriginal students some good. Later on, when I had those white students on clinical up in Brewarrina for three weeks they learned so much. Their attitudes changed. They loved it. They didn't want to leave.

I think the issue of using Aboriginal facilities is a critical one. If courses are going to attract more Aboriginal students then one of the carrots would be to provide opportunities for clinical practice in Aboriginal centres, units and schools. Both Aboriginal and non-Aboriginal students should attend these placements. They might then find out about some of the real problems facing my people. It would also give Aboriginal students a sense of pride and provide our people with role models if they included Aboriginal centres in clinical training. And Aboriginal people would also see mixed groups of students working together and that would help to take away their fear and uncertainty. It might help encourage Aboriginal people to use the mainstream health system for treatment.

Another thing was the travelling or needing overnight accommodation. This was a real problem. I felt more comfortable when we had our own facilitators there because there was a lot of opposition to us from the hospital staff in the early days when I was going through. Some horrendous stories came out about our clinicals. If I'd had no previous experience in hospitals I would have been terrified to set foot in some of those places. Aboriginal kids coming from an Aboriginal environment, they wouldn't even go into such places to be treated, let alone to work. Going into that clinical environment, a white hospital, with white students, and a white facilitator was uncomfortable even for me. It would be really scary for young students from the bush.

They called us the 'peppermint ladies', because we had those green uniforms. They had dreadful stories going around, about the stupid things we were supposed to have done, like a lady wanted a pan in bed, and they put a commode chair on the bed and made her sit on that… They were laughing at us….

Eunice ended up with five bi-passes. She collapsed when she was at Fairfield Hospital and this guy just looked down at her and kept reading his newspaper. We were the first lot of students to be coming out of the university. Older nursing staff were threatened by us and they'd try and put us down. But after we'd been working there for a while, and they saw we were OK, we were always welcomed back. We just persevered. But those first initial clinicals were very difficult; we nearly gave up.

You had to write it all down and be very clear what your procedures would be. I remember one of the charge nurses, she was fairly senior in the ward, she took my nursing care plans, and showed it to the doctor, expecting him to ridicule them. He said, 'This is great.' Shot her down in flames.

Later, if I found a patient whom I instinctively knew felt uncomfortable with me I would go out of my way to let them see that I was as capable as any one else. They'd ring the bell. You could see a look of utter horror on their faces, that I was coming in to see what they needed. I would go out of my way, I'd really crawl to them. Three days later, they'd ring the bell, and they'd say, 'We want the dark one.'

The staff didn't look at me as an Aboriginal but as a student who wanted to learn, was willing to take part. If they did see me as an Aboriginal it was mostly because they wanted to know more about our ways and our culture.

I was somehow determined to get through that course. Maybe I'm just that little bit luckier because through my whole life I've said, I can't let the system beat me. That was one goal which never changed. But without the Aboriginal Liaison Unit at Macarthur it would have been a lot tougher. To be able to go in there and feel that was my community. Not that they could help much with nursing studies, but it was just that feeling of belonging there. I felt very safe in that place, if things were worrying me or I had a particular problem I'd stay there for hours just cursing, but I felt safe and so that kept me going. We'd be sitting in the Unit and we'd be nearly crying one minute and then we'd be laughing. But if it hadn't been for Jane Perkiss, our tutor, she kept us going.

That's the good thing about Koori communities. I could go anywhere and in five minutes fit in and feel at home. We noticed when white people came into the Unit that they didn't know anything. When they first came in they felt very uncomfortable and we would torment them sometimes. To be able to laugh and get it all out and tease each other, it's good. We laughed so much down there – but we cried a lot too.

One time, I'd come to see Judith and she'd thought I was going to ask for another extension. But what I was going to tell her was how I'd made a book on career pathways for anybody who was going to go into Aboriginal Nursing, with some of the things that they should be watching out for. I had photos in it and had printed it all up. I'd done it in the colours and done a drawing on it. All I needed was some black tape to run down the back, I only had green.

As I came towards her she said, 'This is not Koori time.'

'This is not Koori time!' Having a go at me for being late.

I said 'Well forget it then. I was just coming to tell you I was going over to buy some black tape but I won't buy it now, I'll put green on it.' I took it up to her and put it in. And she's sitting there with a grin on her face.

She'd never had contact with Aboriginal people before. This is why I love Judith. Because she was willing to learn, and be open-minded. She'd say, 'Gee, they're noisy Nance.' I'd say, 'Well, if you think they're noisy there, you should go up and sit around the fire bucket with them on the mission!'

The first time she came into the Aboriginal unit, do you know what she did? I purposely did it to her, I shouldn't have done it. I got her a chair that sank down, you know, when you sit on it and it sinks. I shouldn't have done it. So she comes in and she's got her cup for her cup of tea, see, and I said, 'Sit down over there.' and she's looking around. And I said, 'Yeah, there's spears on the wall there.' The bitch I am. So, she goes over to the seat and she sits down and sinks down.

Well she jumps straight up and I knew that was the reaction I'd get. I turned around and said, 'Well now, what's the matter Judith?' 'Oh nothing, nothing.' But she was willing to do something about her view of Aborigines. Now, she's great. She's great. She was funny.

The day that I got word that Ruby wanted to meet me at Bourke, I ran in there, I was so excited. I was deciding what to do. Judith was there, she came and grabbed my arm and gave me a big hug and squashed my glasses right over across my face, and held me that tight I could hardly breathe. I'm thinking, I'm not going to get up to Ruby. I'm not going to get there.

When she finally let me go, I said, 'I've got to let Betty know. I wonder if Betty will let me go.'

And this other one said, 'Of course she will. Betty's always cared for natives.'

I thought to myself, you bitch. I'm glad I didn't answer that now. I would've been only lowering myself right down. That one had a way to belittle me, to try to make me feel that big.

When I was young I always felt I had to feel thankful for what they'd done for me. It was a terrible feeling, it just got hammered in. You have to be grateful. You ungrateful child! How many times had I heard this in my young life? You were more or less brainwashed into feeling that you had to be grateful.

It wasn't until I was at University that I thought to myself one day, what am I doing with my life? What? I was still standing with my hands behind my back and my head down when I was talking to a white person. Judith used to grab me by the head and say, 'What are you doing?' I didn't realise I was almost touching my forehead on my chest.

Working within the Aboriginal community

Immediately after her graduation in May 1988, Nancy took up a position in an Aboriginal health centre in Brewarrina, a small town in outback New South Wales. Within a short time Nancy's skills and talent were widely recognised. She was invited by the then Minister of Health to take up a ministerial position as a member of the Nurses Registration Board in New South Wales. In this role she would represent the voice of her people.

Because of the kinship and community connectedness when something happens to one member, the whole of the population is affected. Take the black death in custody when I was up in Brewarrina. Immediately when the boy burst in and said Uncle Lloyd Boney has been found hanged, I felt sick personally. I was just going to eat my tea. I put my knife and fork down and thought why is this little kid, just a youngster, telling us this. His mother came out and just looked at him. Soon everybody in that house was disturbed, and then the whole community heard the word and there were clusters and clusters of people just standing around trying to understand. Then everybody went up to town to check it out. The family was about the last one to be told about it.

There was a big feeling of panic, disbelief, anger and other things going on. Lloyd Boney's family came around to the Health Centre later. I said for them to come round there so they could sit and talk. I felt they had to talk, this family, and let out what they were feeling. So round they came and we talked and talked.

But Aboriginal families are not just mum, dad and the kids. The room was packed with everybody who could say 'I'm family'. There was this big mob of people and I felt overwhelmed by it. I kept going, trying to support the group, but I rang 400 km away to Dubbo to get help. I asked for a psychologist and two counsellors to come up and help me, but nobody came. Nobody came. And it ended up with a riot – the whole town got angry. People somehow had to get rid of this hopeless feeling of being unwanted.

I get emotional when I talk about it because I know how these people were feeling and even when I go up now five or six years after that event I like to go round and see his dad. Mum and dad are separated, the family is split up, they still haven't come to terms with what happened. I'm still counselling these people. The need doesn't go away. The need for this family to get ongoing help and support and the need for the rest of Australians to understand how devastating that is to an Aboriginal family. It's affecting that town even now. That's a long time and the poor old dad, his anger is still intense and he talks so quickly when he gets angry that you can't understand him properly. That's happening all over and I think non-Aboriginal health care staff must realise that they will probably come up against it again.

We had an Aboriginal boy with a diagnosed mental disorder living in Brewarrina where a non-Aboriginal person stepped in and didn't even consult with Aboriginal staff. The boy was sent 400 km away – to give Mum some respite. What happened was, he committed suicide because he was taken away from his family. Now there's a whole lot of feelings of guilt and anger there, and blame.

We have to consult with the family. It's really important with any people with a mental problem. You'll probably find there's a whole lot of people happy to take that boy down to their place while mum goes away for a week or so, instead of sending him away to be locked up. He perceived that he was totally cut off and forgotten, which couldn't be further from the truth.

In Brewarrina my time was not structured. There was a certain order, chaotic order, but in the mainstream it was do this and then this and the boss would have a fit if things weren't done by a certain time. Out there I certainly had goals for each day. I would have a diabetes day and that would mean I'd be going round seeing all my diabetics and checking their medication, making sure their feet were all right or that their diet was okay. But you could get turned away from that schedule at any time.

I used to look at the staff in our regular community centre and see them so ordered, so neat and tidy, but my clinic wasn't. I would be giving sex talks to the boys down on the riverbank, or talking to the mums sitting on the verandah while they were playing bingo and we'd be talking about food or such, between the numbers of course, but it was all very informal. If something came up and you saw the opening you grabbed your chance with both hands. But I noticed that a lot of my people still have a mission mentality, that when they were buying their food they'd go for the flour, sugar and tea, big bags of flour, big bags of sugar, cheap. It's the way they were brought up and they weren't about to change until we got round to talking about nutrition for the kids. All they were thinking was fill the belly. You can't tell Koori people what to do, just give them the information of what's available. Too many years of being told you have to do this or that, I suppose.

Some of them don't care, but a lot of it is still resentment of those years, that history of neglect and dislocation. But as an Aborigine and a nurse when I see them drinking, see the apathy, hear them say they can't be bothered or what's the good of it, I start thinking - hey we've got to make these people think they are worthwhile. A lot of them have the idea that they are not good enough. Some of them don't want to change either, they cling to the past, particularly the older ones. They're quite happy to live on the reserve and I don't think they should be made to go away from that, ever. They have their set rules and their way of life. For years and years they've walked to the Centre to get their water and walked home with it. They built all these flash homes at Bourke reserve and what happened? People still had to walk to the Centre to get their water because the builders didn't put water into the houses. Just little things.

A lot of Aboriginal people don't know the difference between being angry and being assertive. They are either passive or aggressive, they don't feel confident enough in their ability to be assertive. I tried to tell them how they could be assertive in the face of criticism, to get them to say, 'Excuse me that is wrong and I don't have to take that from you', and not be rude and go punch them in the nose. That behaviour caused a lot of bad blood between them and the hospital staff. We've got to stop these people feeling bad, but nobody ever tells them how to change.

For instance when the young girls went to hospital they didn't have pretty nighties or night things and felt they were not able to disagree or ask questions. But I did teach the young mums one trick to help them to take control. They learned to say, 'When's my baby going to have its hepatitis B injection?' They would come home and report that when they said that the nurse stopped and looked at them with more respect. Feeling hopeless has been a big part of Aboriginal people's lives and once we start getting rid of that they will be ready to listen to what we say as far as their physical health goes.

Working in Sydney

After Brewarrina, Nancy returned to Sydney in 1990 and worked in a mainstream psychiatric hospital, Cumberland Hospital, which specialised in the drug and alcohol field. In particular, they were developing programs of care and rehabilitation for Aboriginal people. Her stories are drawn from her first-hand experience of being an Aboriginal woman who was now living and working closely among her own people.

When I first went to Brewarrina as a new graduate I wondered whether I would make a difference. I suppose I was as naive as everyone else who has tried to work with Kooris. I thought that because I was Aboriginal they would listen to me, but I was wrong. These people don't accept anybody until they prove themselves worthy of trust. To them I was still the registered nurse who had come to 'solve' their problems. When they found out that I hadn't lost sight of who I was and where I was from they started to warm up. And they'd still come to me with problems later when I went up to visit my family. My people down there on Dodge (the reserve) who used to be sitting with a flagon were sitting with a bottle of water with them. When I asked what it was, they said so proudly, 'Water'. They are 60 years old and had probably been drinking all their lives and here they are drinking water with their grog. To maintain their hydration and make them feel good about their lives is real progress.

When I worked on Dodge I was a completely different person. Different set of behaviours, a different world. I'm not saying that I acted in a less professional way when I was working there but probably it was less formal than down here. In a mainstream hospital you are in nice clean shoes and stockings and the uniform always pressed. Your presentation was expected to be first class. Up there I could slop around in a pair of old jeans and shoes and not worry because I was doing what everyone else was doing. Of course there were rules and standards which I maintained. But I was my own boss and I could set my own times. Sometimes I got opposition not from the non-Aboriginal but from the Aboriginal people. When that started to happen I'd feel down because they've got to see that health is not just a bandaid and a needle in the bum, it's a lot more and they need to understand the concept of preventative health.

At first the management tried to model our Aboriginal health centre on what they could see the white centre doing. That is, providing white medicine, acute care, and high technology interventions. My plan was totally different. I wanted the people to have a place they would feel comfortable coming to and we could work in a different way. But people on the committee of the health centre, they thought it would be good if we were doing everything the white fella was doing. I tried to tell them but they could only see that I was trying to turn it into an amusement centre, according to them. I don't know if they were quite ready for my ideas of Aboriginal health practices. I think I had a broader, more flexible view of the world and knew what was possible. It was probably too simple. It was radical, but it looked too simple. There was no mystery about it, just good common sense and maybe that was the problem, that it wasn't all mysterious like the white centre. That's why we need to encourage students to come to Aboriginal communities for their practicums and see how it really is.

When I was working in Bre, I worked very long hours, with constant put downs and criticism from the non-Aboriginal people. I was working very hard with the Aboriginal people. In the end I got burnt out and so decided to come back to Sydney.

I then got a job at Wisteria House. At first I learned a great deal about punctuality, confidentiality, professionalism and documentation. Everything I learned in my course at university just fell into place because that was the environment for which students were being prepared. I was able to function readily as one of the team. But then I found myself being used as an Aboriginal educator for the non-Koori staff because we were getting more and more Kooris in when they heard there was a Koori working on staff. More Kooris were coming into the detoxification unit and the Nurse Unit Manager could see the need for education and the staff were asking all these questions. So I became an in-service educator for the staff. While it's great to work with Aboriginal people in their environment and that gives certain freedom and flexibility, it also means there's a lack of infrastructure and mechanisms for such things as staff development and regular in-service to educate staff to different methods of care. I felt that what I was doing was worthwhile.

When I first went to the hospital, part of my job was working in the detox unit and then the rehabilitation unit, getting the chronic alcoholics into some sort of routine, using activities of daily living – get up, dressed, make your bed, go out have your tea, do this, do that. They were so frightened. We would get them into a routine, so they could perhaps move into a house. It was good work and I probably needed this period to adjust, to see how the system functioned, and to learn my way around and feel comfortable, but these were non-Aboriginal people. Then I particularly asked to work in the drug and alcohol unit because I felt that I needed to upgrade all my skills and knowledge. I know a certain amount of what happens with drugs and withdrawal but I wanted to learn the details. My people have a problem with these things. It was after I found one of my friends tied down on the bed one time – not at this hospital – that I felt there must be alternatives for my people. But without more experience I didn't feel confident.

At the same time I was also dealing with the Kooris who came in with their mental health problems. I know that using alcohol and drugs was the outcome of their problems. It was a symptom of other social, economic and self-esteem issues. So we set up a small study and went back over the records. For some time now people have been identified when they go into hospital as to whether they are Aboriginal. So we went back two or three years and looked at all the Aboriginal admissions. We particularly looked at how long they stayed. We found that over this period about 15 or 16 had been admitted. Of these admissions, 11 left the next day, one stayed for three weeks, one stayed to detox properly, and another one stayed about three days. But a high percentage of people who came in stayed the night and left. Only one person in all that time actually completed the program. It was obvious that the method of treatment and care was not appropriate and was functioning poorly.

So I used the information we'd gathered to put a case to the hospital management that they weren't giving the care my people needed. I made a few suggestions which were adopted and we started to introduce some small changes in the method of care. This included the in-service program, of course. For a start, when Aboriginal people were admitted and saw me displaying my colours (the red, black and yellow), it put them at ease. For example, we had one big guy come in and he was really uptight. So I said, 'Let's go out and walk by the river.' Kooris are much better able to talk and be calm if they can get outside in the fresh air and not be closed in. So there we were walking up and down. We calmed him down and then as a team listened to his problems and discussed his needs for care and support. In the end he went on through the program. He came to visit me the other day and he'd been two years free of alcohol. This is a guy who'd been classed by the other Aboriginal people as a no-hoper, but here he was. The difference in his face, his appearance was wonderful. It was so rewarding to see the change in both the staff and the person. As a team we did a lot of talking and experimenting with care approaches. Of course, it didn't always work out that well.

The Aboriginal people that I found most difficult to get to really look at their problems were the older ones. These were the ones who'd been taken from their families, raised on the missions and were totally confused about their identity and where they belonged. They were shutting it out completely, they wouldn't talk about it. In the hospital they'd do as they were told because that's how they were brought up, but as soon as they were discharged they'd go out and use again. They have to get all that out, being in the homes, taken away from their families. Until they can do that they'll never be any good and no matter what care we provide it will be less than successful. So skills in counselling and support are essential. But direct counselling methods such as those you can use with white people won't work with Aboriginal people. You have to be much less direct, talk around the problem, pretend to talk about something else which is easier and safer. Otherwise these old ones won't talk at all, it's too painful.

The best way to get a black talking is to say where you are from. They'll know someone from the area. You can get them going and before they know it you've got them in the palm of your hand. They think you're interested in them and can't be too bad. So just little things. I was really lucky to be there at that time and be able to educate those people properly. Now those staff are educated about what's going on and I don't have to be there all the time. I can become a resource, they know they can call on me, but they will educate others and feel confident about dealing with Aboriginal people.

Some of the staff were particularly receptive. Bob and Caroline, for example, became really strong advocates of the need for non-Aboriginal people to listen and become aware. They were two of my strongest allies and friends. They still are. They worked with me. Bob grew up in an entirely redneck environment. He'd probably be the first to tell you that. He is a wonderful person, and that was because we had the chance to work this way. I think Cumberland Hospital was wonderful, and should be commended on the ways they used this opportunity to have in-service training and other courses.

Finding Ruby

In 1980 I was down at the old Mark Foys building to see about a place for us. The Department of Housing used to be in there. I was going to see about getting a house. They said to me, 'Mr Edwards will take you up to the big boss.' Mr Edwards, who was an Aboriginal man, took me all the way up to the boss's office. I was so anxious about getting the house that I didn't even ask him if he knew Ruby Edwards. He stood on one side of the lift and we didn't say a word to each other.

It wasn't 'til three days later , when I was packing to go to this new house that I started screaming, 'Aaaah!'

My little kids all come running down, 'What's the matter, Mum?'

'A Mr Edwards! That's our family name! He took me up to the housing office and he had curly hair! Like me!'

What do you do? All those years of searching and there I was, thrown together with an Aboriginal guy with curly hair who had the name of Edwards – and I didn't even ask him. It was so funny.

I rang Housing to find out where he was, 'Oh yeah, Sonny. Sonny's gone on holidays'. I thought, 'Oh'. And this person on the phone, he said 'Why?' I explained to this guy and he rang Dubbo airport, got Sonny to ring me. 'Did you want to speak to me?' he said.

'Look, all I want to know is, do you know a Ruby Edwards?'

'Yes,' he said, 'That's my aunt. She lives in Pine St, Wallsend, Newcastle.'

All those years I'd been asking Aboriginal people all over if they knew Ruby Edwards.

My mother, my beautiful mother, all my life I'd been thinking how much I loved her.

Where are you? I'm thinking of you today, I'm looking at a particular spot, and thinking, I'll remember this moment for the rest of my life and I'm saying to you that I love you …

I can remember those times. Sunny days, windy days. Always, always thinking about my mother.

You grow up with this.

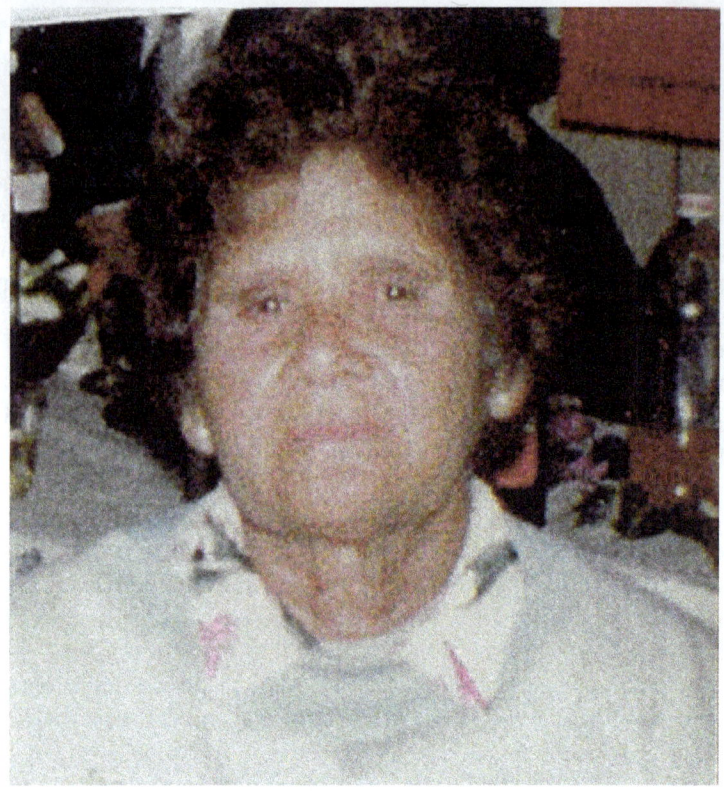

Nancy's only photo of her mother, Ruby. Photographer unknown.

And now, I had finally found my family.

In my excitement I went to the Salvation Army and got them to go around and speak to her. When they got there, she said, 'No, no, that can't be right. She's not my daughter, you're wrong.' They said she was shaking and crying and wouldn't look at them. She didn't want anything to do with me. I thought, back off, Nance. Back off.

Next I rang my friend, an Aboriginal health worker in Newcastle. She agreed to meet me and take me out there. I said my name was Mary Harris. Mary was my best friend. We went to Ruby's house and she invited us in. My friend was asking her how was she going? How's things? How's Crow? And going on about the whole family.

Ruby got up and left the room and went out into the kitchen. While she was out I took off my sunglasses. When she returned, she sat down in the chair next to me. She glanced at me, and immediately noticed my light coloured eyes. Her look of astonishment was enough for me. She said to my friend, 'Have you heard from that girl who's looking for her mother?'

Next thing she's getting all these cuttings out and showing them to me: Crow got an award for bravery. Some other kid played cricket for Australia, and all this.

As I was leaving, she said, 'You will come back and see me, won't you babe?' I said, 'Yes, I will.' But I let it go then. Later she moved back up to Bourke.

It was after I joined Link Up in 1984, four years later, that Coral and Peter got me to write a letter telling her everything I wanted her to know. I told her that I understood, that I loved her and I told her all about my family. But I didn't put anything about the pain. I think she was well aware of that. Peter and Coral took the letter up to give it to her and she wasn't going to take it. Oh, no. Then she said, 'Give it to me', and stuck it in her bag. Cousins have told me that she read it over and over again.

I did not hear from Ruby again until 1986 when Ruby rang Link Up. She asked if they could contact me and asked if I could come and visit her.

The day I found out my mother wanted to see me, actually wanted to meet me, I was at Uni. I ran up to the main office in Nursing so I could ring up to organise the trip. I couldn't get on a plane. Couldn't get on a train. It must have been a long weekend – I couldn't get on anything to get to Bourke. I must have eventually got a ticket for the Thursday. I remember I had a tutorial to do and Eunice, my beautiful friend, she's since died, she had to give my tute paper for me.

Because you have to leave at 7.30 in the morning, of course I had all this time to think about it. The enormity of the whole situation. You get to Dubbo and you've only got a few minutes break there and you're all herded into a coach and off you go again. Then at 4.30 you stop at Nyngan and have a cup of tea. Then you get up to Coolabah and you stop again and have a drink and stretch your legs.

The amazing landscapes you go through! That's when you feel how wonderful Australia is. And for me to suddenly come to grips with the fact that this is my country, this is where my people belong, this land. That's pretty touching. To suddenly be looking at the land in a different light.

This was interspersed with all this doubt that I had. Of course, by the time we got to Coolabah it was getting pretty dark. You're winging along there and I thought, Byrock is the next stop, I'll get out at Byrock. It's no good, it's not going to work. But we were running a bit late so the bus driver says, 'Nobody for Byrock, right?' and we went straight through. We kept on going.

I was sitting there and there was a moon shining, it must have been a full moon because I could see quite clearly the shapes and trees – just wonderful. I remember seeing the mountain at Bourke, it's a big flat top mountain. It was very beautiful that night, with the moon shining and me seeing Mount Oxley. Then in the distance you could see the lights of Bourke shining, it was way in the distance and it seemed to be forever before you got there. Nobody else on the bus knew what I was thinking, what I was feeling.

I got to Bourke. When we got to the bus stop, I got off and Dolly was waiting there for me. Dolly Bates. She was a graduate from Bathurst, I think she did teaching, Teacher Ed. She was a Link Up person and she was looking for her daughter. After a long trip, you know, you are so tired. But when she said, 'Now do you want to go and have a cup of tea first or go out and see Aunty Tiny now?' – Aunty Tiny, that's what they called Ruby – I said, 'I want to go now.'

Link Up Services

Today, Link Up services are organisations funded by the Aboriginal and Torres Strait Islander Commission (ATSIC) 'to assist with the process of family tracing and reunion ... for Aboriginal and Torres Strait Islander people who, as children, were separated from their families by compulsion, duress or undue influence under the past laws, practices and policies of the Commonwealth, State and Territory Governments'. With the objective of facilitating family reunions for 'Indigenous people removed as children, families searching for children removed, and foster and adoptive families', Link Up undertakes the research needed to access

Finding Ruby

family and personal records, obtain copies of records, provide support and advice in relation to such records, locate family members, arrange and assist with family reunions, provide support and counselling prior to, during and after family reunions, including grief and loss counselling and assistance with building relationships (see the *Bringing Them Home* report page on the ATSIC web site: www.atsic.gov.au)

Link Up was started in the early 1980s by Coral Edwards, an Aboriginal woman who had been removed from her family as a child and returned home as an adult, and Peter Read, an historian who had been carrying out exhaustive research on the history of the stolen generations. Together they set up Link Up (NSW) Aboriginal Corporation, aiming to help other Aboriginal people who had been removed from families and communities to find their way back home (Read 1999:70). It was supported from the beginning by grants from Federal and State governments. It is now a nation-wide non-profit organisation whose membership, full-time staff and governing body are all Aboriginal people who were separated from their families as children (Edwards and Read 1989:xviii).

Peter Read recalls that during Link Up's early days, the removal of children was rarely mentioned within Aboriginal communities. It was still seen to somehow reflect badly on the people and families whose children had been taken away. Aboriginal communities themselves still seemed to have no idea '*why or how so many of their children had been removed*' (Read 1999:101) and were not aware that their removal had been the result of specific government policies. Coral and Peter began their work by bringing the history of removal to light. They were able to let Aboriginal communities know that children hadn't been 'given away' by their mothers, as they had generally been told. They could also tell them that those children who had been removed and had not returned had not done so because they were ashamed of their families, but as a result of the ways in which they had been indoctrinated and lied to. They had not known who to turn to to help them find their way home. Link Up's primary purpose was – and is – to find out where their client's families were living, to organise a meeting between their client and their client's family, and to help them maintain contact with each other (Read 1999:71–72).

Read explains that one of the ways that Link Up has helped the people who come to them has been through educating them about the real reasons for their removal. Many Aboriginal people grew up believing that they had been given away because their families had not wanted them. To be told that it was more likely that they had been removed against their parents' wishes, whether under some Act or law or by means of threat, pressure or persuasion, has been enough to give many people the courage to seek out the families they had lost. Often, details of their removal were first revealed to them through access to official government files held in the State Archives. These often held other previously unknown information about their families (Read 1999:78).

As well as the fear of rejection, many of Link Up's clients grew up with such negative images of Aboriginality that it has been very difficult for them to overcome their own fears and prejudices and enter the unfamiliar Aboriginal environments of their families. Link Up assists these clients through counselling, in particular urging them to try and withhold judgments about their families, their homes and lifestyles until they have had time to get to know more about them (Read 1999: 93).

Every one of Link Up's clients has a different story and different experiences of the reunion process. Link Up aims to meet these different needs. They help provide information about family and personal history by obtaining the files of the Aborigines Protection Board and Aborigines Welfare Board, which may include personal letters and photos as well as official documents. If possible, Link Up contacts the family member who is being sought and tries to set up a meeting. They accompany their client to the meeting, assist with the reunion process by following up with counselling and advice about how to deal with the reunion and its aftermath, and help organise support groups (Read 1999:72–100).

In the mirror

Her flat backed into a lane. I could hardly walk. I could hardly walk. I know why she was sitting down when I arrived, because she probably felt the same way. There were all these people around. I thought, I can't believe this! All your life, you go through your life not looking like anybody, or you see someone that does look sort of similar and you think, 'I wonder, I wonder if ...'

But to sit there and look at her. The first thing I noticed was her dark eyes, mine are light. I was so much like my Ruby. It was unbelievable, unbelievable to sit there and to actually look at her after all those years. There she was. A mirror. A mirror.

We were sitting at this table, with people all around, and there was this old white woman there. But I think my mother must have had eyes in the back of her head, because every time that old white woman tried to look at me, she'd move her head this way or that, so that white woman, she couldn't see.

I think my mother knew when she looked at me.

Crow, my brother, was looking through the servery, there was a little servery window, and he's leaning on that, a big, big man, looking at me through that, not saying anything. I thought, 'Gee, I'm not going to tangle with him, he's such a big bloke', you know. She's talking to me, a whole lot of nonsense, the conversation was making no sense. I thought, 'Oh God, let me out of here', that sort of thing.

Crow went into his room and Dolly went after him and said, 'Well what do you think, Crow?' And he said, 'I'll tell you one thing, she's a bloody Edwards.' I heard later that, after I left that night, he was lying on his bed and he was saying in a sing song voice, 'Ruby's been telling me lies.' Ruby'd said to him, 'Shut up Crow or I'll throw you out of this house.' So he knew. Crow has always been big. Crow has always been feisty. Always.

To grow up, not knowing your family, you don't know who you look like, you know. To suddenly sit in front of somebody and it was almost like looking in a mirror, although she had dark eyes and I have light eyes. To look at her full on in the face like that, I can't describe it. But I still wasn't getting the reaction that I needed.

'No, no,' she said, 'do I look like a woman who would give my child away?' No, of course my mother didn't 'give me away'. But she was full of denial. She could not bring herself to accept me as her daughter.

Later, we decided to go and spend the night at Ruby's sister's house, to spend the night down there, so we could talk. We spent the night there. Gladys, Ruby and myself. The next morning, as we walked back to Ruby's flat, we were walking up this laneway, just the two of us, nobody around and she could just be who she wanted to be. She came and put her arm through mine and never said a word. Never said a word, but she was holding on to me tightly. When I told the girls they said, 'Geez, that's not like Mama.' I knew then that she was letting me know.

But I just loved it when she'd say to them, 'That old woman's not my baby.' I wasn't. I wasn't the baby she lost. I was an old woman. God love her – I wasn't that bloody old!

The next day, I was walking up the main road and I could feel everybody looking at me. Dolly said to me, 'Can you feel that everybody's looking at you?' I said, 'Yes I can, I feel awful.' She said, 'Don't worry about it, they're all your rellies.' That did something to me then.

We went down to the weir. She wanted to show me the Darling River, to have a look at the river. Nowadays it's hard to even find the river, it's not that wide – it's the cotton farms. Anyway, crossing the weir there was a whole lot of Aboriginal people sitting with fishing poles. I think we all love fishing, see, we're fishing mad. I dunno how many of them were lined up on that weir fishing. Dolly said, 'They're all your rellies too.' I looked across and sure enough they're all yapping to each other about us, getting really carried away.

Every time I walked up and down the road, they were all looking at me. They were my relatives. I had one old white man come up to me in Bourke and shake me by the hand, saying, 'I'm so sorry to hear about Archie dying.' I'm looking at him! Then he grinned, 'Oh, I'm sorry.' He thought I was Ruby. He thought I was Ruby – and he'd lived in Bourke all his life.

I walked into a TAFE class where all my aunties, well, not all, there were 14 of them altogether, but quite a few, were getting taught by one of my cousins. Dolly took me there so I could meet them. They said to me after, 'We got such a shock when you walked into that room.' My second youngest sister, she said to me later, 'You're so much like Mum when she was younger.'

I used to think about my mother on my birthdays. I would think about her. Like all children, you think special things at a very special moment. You think 'I'm doing this' or 'I'm doing that.' I was that sort of child, a dreamer. I remember this day I was in Bidura. I was standing inside and out there it was a beautiful day. I'm looking up and I'm thinking, 'Today, now, it's my birthday and I'm standing here and I'm thinking especially about my mother.'

Years later when I found my mother, my sisters, they said to me, 'When it was Johnny's birthday' – Johnny's my younger brother – 'round his birthday Mama used to cry all the time, she'd cry.' I said, 'When's John's birthday?' They said, 'On the 9th of March.' 'Well, mine's on the 11th!' I said. The girls would say, 'Why are you crying, Mum, why are you crying?' She'd look into space and say,

'Oh nothing, oh nothing.' Just the knowledge that she was actually thinking of me around the same time I was sending that message out to her made me feel a little better about my life. I knew her love had been reaching out to me.

Now growing up all these years, you think of these movies that you see where people run towards each other, you know, and it's just so wonderful. Well this was the big dream I had. But Mum and I ran towards each other and we missed each other completely.

She could not think of me as the baby she lost. 'That old woman's not my baby', she'd say to the rest of the family.

Rejection again

My poor old darling mother. All those years she'd probably felt such a guilt that you would not understand, and now it must all have surfaced. Fancy having that on your mind, all those years and you can't talk to anybody about it.

One of the highlights of this visit to Bourke was spending the night with my mother. We were spending the night at my Auntie Gladys's house. That was the highlight. We went down to Gladys's place. Gladys had no kids there, they were all married. We had spent that night down at Auntie Gladys's place and then we had breakfast together. This was a strange time. I'd say something, and Gladys would look at my mother, straight at Ruby, and my mother wouldn't move a muscle. She was a tough old bird, I tell you.

We didn't go to sleep. It was an amazing night. Just ten hours in my whole life I spent with my mother.

Thank God she was tough. I reckon it was her genes that got me through my life. Her tenacity. She worked hard all her life. She rarely missed a day at work. She was highly respected by the Aboriginal and the non-Aboriginal community. And then to have to say, 'This is my daughter that was taken away.' The shame that seemed to be associated with that.

I can understand. No one can make up for what happened.

One of Ruby's friends said to me later, 'Why doesn't that bloody old goat just own up that she's got you.' I said, 'Don't talk about her like that!' I couldn't hassle her, because I had to stop and think, what did she go through? She had ten kids after that and they never got another one off her. Feisty old darling she was. They went droving. They did everything. They used to camp out west. There's a story about Aboriginal people and the life they lived out west and it mentions the Edwards' camp. That's where my Mum grew up, amongst those people there. They used to go droving and doing all these things to avoid the government man coming along and grabbing the kids. They never got another one of hers.

But they took me away, and others – they said, 'to give us a better life'. Dear God! I'd love to get behind Senator Herron, would I love to get behind him. How dare they say that it was to give me a better life. When I got home I find that two other members of my family are actually registered nurses. They're working in social welfare, they're working in all these things, with the same feelings as me, the same longings as me. We love the same country and western music, classical music, you know. Quite mad the lot of them, like me. So, I mean, how dare they say they took me away and put my mother and I through all of this hell to give me a better life. They didn't. They didn't.

They gave me a hell of a life, a lonely, horrible life.

The next generation

My youngest son, David went up to Bourke. This story of mine, it doesn't affect me only. It affects the whole community. It affects all my family. My children got all excited but when David went up, Ruby slammed the door in his face. Crow was there doing the gardening and he said, 'I'm sorry mate. Are you all right?' He said 'Yeah', and he went. He didn't realise then it was Crow.

I said, 'What did you do?' He said, 'I went down to the river and cried, Mum'.

Then a few years later after we'd moved up there to live at Brewarrina, David was in the pub at Bourke and he was talking to this bloke. He didn't realise it was Crow. Kevin Knight, he's me cuz, came in and he said to David, 'David, do you realise that that's your uncle?' And David cried. Twenty-six and he cried. So what's it been doing to my family too?

My Peter never married. He went out with one white girl and one Aboriginal girl. The Aboriginal girl married another bloke and the other girl, they just broke up. But he never ever got really close to anybody else again. He'd meet these nice Koori girls, you know, and I'd think, oh, he might, you know. He said to me, 'No, I was frightened, Mum. I was frightened I might marry a sister or a cousin or something like that, you know. I couldn't'.

We went up to meet my younger sister, Ducky, who's a registered nurse too. She's a year younger than my Peter. Peter said, 'I tell you what, I could've gone for her.' A beautiful looking girl. He said, 'What if I'd gone for her, Mum?' He was just letting me know that this is how he's felt it.

He's led a very lonely life I think, my Peter. He devoted his life to Megan and David when I was on my own. He looked after them when I went to university. He is now the surrogate father for all these grandkids of mine. I can never tell him really how much I love him or am thankful to him for what he's done. But I do believe his life is messed up because of the policies of the government of the day which took me away from my Mum. It has carried on down to him.

I'm damn sure that it's not going to happen again, that those policies are not going to interfere with my grandchildren's lives. I'm trying to teach them and tell them all these things I've been talking about here so that when they grow up, they're going to be proud members of the Australian community. But they're also going to be very proud of their Aboriginality.

She was a good mum. Dirt poor but apparently the kids always had a feed, always clean, you know. She must have had strong morals and ethics about life, about how we live, how we look after ourselves, how we treat other people, because all, all those people are the same. My Aunt Nita, she's just beautiful to me. When I met her, I walked in and they reckon their mouths dropped open! But they never said a word. Nita has been so beautiful to me. She's my aunt - Ruby's sister. It was Ruby's stepfather who was an Edwards. Somebody said to me that Ruby was a West from South Queensland. There's a lot of Wests out there, south west, out towards Quilpie, but we don't know for sure. In Evelyn Crawford's book, she talks about Yantabulla, the Edwards' camp. Well that was my old grandfather's camp and that's where they say my mother got pregnant, at Yantabulla. I'm not really interested in my father. But I know that Ruby was sent away. There seem to be a few stories that might have circulated. Did she give the story out that my father and she, this is all very romantic, met on the banks of the Murray and I was conceived, and that he came from Dalgety, or Diligen, and that he was a Richards?

Around Dalgety they deny ever knowing a Ruby. They never knew her. So I reckon that the old grandfather and the old publican at Yantabulla, who apparently respected the old grandfather very much, cooked up a story linked to the Murray River. Old grandfather and the family always used to go down fruit picking, working all along the Murray there. They knew all these people, and they put these people into my story.

I had a letter from the welfare writing to a Mrs Rutherford at Dalgety asking did they know where Ruby was. They'd never even heard of her. So these people, even though they're written into my story, they didn't know Ruby.

I think the people that sent Ruby to Sydney so that she could have the baby helped to fix up a story because they knew who my father was. My father could have been anybody, we don't know. It was all covered up. Very, very covered up. If it had been another black fella, they wouldn't have covered it up, would they? I think they tried to get me away to keep things quiet and that's how Ruby ended up in Sydney.

You look forward to meeting your Mum all those years and then to be rejected once again. When my sister started to reject me too, I sat there and I thought 'Well, hang about, what am I doing? I am not going to put up with this rejection any more. I know who I am. I met Ruby. I'm satisfied with my identity, so I don't have to have permission from anybody in this world to tell me who I am and who I'm not, and who I belong to and who I don't belong to'.

I like to think that though she could never accept me she was very proud of me, that I'd become the daughter she'd have wanted me to be.

I just made up my mind. I made up my mind when she died. I am not going to have this sort of shit in my life anymore. That's all there is to it. Some of my sisters, even though I don't know them properly

– but I do because they're my flesh and blood – they make me think to myself, 'You're still doing what the government wanted you to do, wanted us to do. They divided us, divide and conquer.' That's what Howard's so busy trying to do at the moment. Divide and conquer. I'm really angry with him.

How many graduates have you had from my family! They were all there, learning, getting into positions to help people, and believe me, they do. I was outside of the circle of family, but still doing the same thing. Isn't it amazing?

So, they didn't win. The system didn't win. I ended up doing exactly what my mother would have wanted me to do.

You ought to hear Doodie, my younger sister, sing. I could sing when I was younger. Of course, I can't now since I had the hysterectomy and since I got sick. I had a high voice, a soprano. I sang on Young Australia once. Doodie's got a powerful voice. She's a singer and loves it. Kevin's musical – they're all musical, they all sing, the whole lot of them. All play an instrument.

Some, not all of them, they like a drink. I say to them, 'I don't think I'll have a charge with you. I'll have a cup of tea but I don't want any grog. But that doesn't mean that I don't want you to have one.' So they feel comfortable about us. Peter doesn't drink and they'll say, 'What are you drinking?' He'll say, 'A straight coke'. But they accept us.

Link Up had published their book and my sisters were reading it. Some in the family were quite angry over it but then decided they wanted to meet me. So we arranged a meeting.

I was going to walk away from my younger sister's house when it came to meeting her. I was so tired of having to justify who I am and I'm not going to do it any more. I'm not. I refuse to do it. I've had enough rejection. I don't want any more. If I have any more, well that's tough.

I got out of the car, and Pete was with me, Peter Read. Thank God for Pete! Carol was with me too. We got out of the car at this nice home, really nice home. I thought, 'Flash black!' I said, 'No, I can't. I really can't do it'. I started to cry and I said to Pete, 'No, I can't, love.' I wanted to turn around and go away.

One life, two stories

> The book Nancy is referring to is *The lost children: thirteen Australians taken from their Aboriginal families tell of the struggle to find their natural parents*. Carol Edwards and Peter Read of Link Up put these stories together, including Nancy's, in 1989.

He said, 'That's all right.' He opened up the car door and wanted me to get back in.

But then Ducky came running out. 'No, no, no! Stay, stay! I know who you are. I know who you are.' When I went to look for my papers to show her, she said, 'I don't want to see them. I know who you are.' Her old man said to her, 'You've only got to look at her nose and your nose.' He's a whitefella.

We have a lot of gestures that are very similar. It was funny looking at her and talking to her because it was sort of looking at me when I was younger. I could see a lot of me there.

I said to a group of school kids I was speaking to one day, that it's funny to suddenly find people that look like you when you grow up in a world of not seeing anybody that looks like you. My kids look like me, David would probably be the one nearest to me, but when I met Ruby she was so much like me to look at that it was spooky. These kids just looked at me. I said, 'You know, when you grow up seeing your mum or your sister or your brother who looks like you all the time you don't take any notice of it. But for me it was the first time'.

I have sat down, I have been crying and I've been leaning against a wall, I can remember sliding down the wall and sitting down with my head in hands just sobbing because what is the use. Why? Why? I couldn't understand it. But then I'd think, 'No! Bugger them!' – you know, I reckon I got that from my poor old mother. She was a tough old bird. She'd go into the girls room and find their beds all made up to look like bodies in the bed and she'd whip back the blankets and it wouldn't be them. They'd be all down the pub having a good old time. She'd go down and get them if they'd been drinking. 'Get your arse home.' She used to round them up. They said she was so tough on them for drinking, because she didn't drink. She was tough on them for their behaviour. She was very well respected in that area by both black and white. I suppose she thought, well if I worked this hard you're not going to muck it up for me.

I'm still being rejected by some of my family. In a way, they put Mum on a pedestal. 'Oh, Mum would have told us about you. Mum would have said something about you.' She couldn't. She couldn't. To her that was a shame thing. A thing to be ashamed about. She took on the whole guilt. She thought that she was guilty because I'd been taken away. She lived all her life with that guilt. Her secret. She didn't tell her family. Half this family of mine – mind you, it's an enormous family – are saying no, and half are saying yes. So I'm still being rejected in a way.

The best thing that happened to me was one Mother's Day when my sister rang me and said, 'Happy Mother's Day'. I'm not used to having calls from my family. In fact, I thought it was one of my best friends, Mary. It just sounded like her. So I'm talking away – thank God I didn't say 'Mary' – and she's talking away and then suddenly, the way the conversation was going, I realised it was my sister who was ringing. I nearly cried. Here was a sister who wanted me, who rang me, who felt the need to ring me and talk to me, who cared about whether I was having a happy mother's day or not. It made up for a lot of things.

It made up for a lot of things.

Being part of the family: Lynette, Nancy's cousin, reflects on what it meant to meet Nancy

It was my elder sister, Yvonne, who first told me about Nancy as she knows a fair bit about our family. One day she said to me, 'Did you know that Aunty Ruby's got another daughter?' and I said no I didn't. She then told me that Aunty Ruby had come down to visit her and it was when they were alone she told Yvonne that Aunty Ruby had shown her a letter which she had received. The letter was from Link Up asking if she was willing to meet Nancy. Yvonne said to her, 'What do you think, Aunty Rube? I think you should, you know. I think you should go down and meet her.'

At the time Aunty Ruby wouldn't admit that Nancy was her daughter but she still kept talking about the letter, and asking whether she should go through with it and make contact.

When I met Nancy I found out that Aunty Ruby ended up ringing Link Up and that's how they met.

When I was living in Bourke, back in 1983 or '84 it must have been and I'd only just come home from living away for a couple of years – I was walking down the main Street in Bourke and I spotted this woman across the road. She was talking to one of my cousins, Robyn Martin. I had to look twice and thought, is that Aunty Ruby? As I got closer I realised that it

One life, two stories

Nancy with Lynette when we were all in Bowral at Pat Bazeley's 'Research Farm' in 2003 working on the book. Photo: Gaynor Macdonald.

wasn't Aunty Ruby, I said 'Oh, I thought you were Aunty Ruby.' And that's when Robyn introduced me, 'This is Nancy, this is Aunty Ruby's daughter.' I said, 'Geez you're the spitting image of her.'

We had a bit of a chat and talked about family then but I didn't see her again until she came back to Bourke some time later. I can't recall whether I was living in Bourke or whether I'd come home for something. Someone contacted me and said, 'Can you come up to the Medical Centre because I've got a lady up here?' I went up and it was Nance. She asked if I would take her to meet some of the family, so we then drove around and went off to meet the family. We called down to Lorraine's (Doodie) house, down near the old Catholic church. Boy (Robert), Doodie (Lorraine) and Crow (Paul) were there at the time (Aunty Ruby's children – Nancy's brothers and sister).

They talked for a while and spoke about different things in general.

I don't know why Nance had asked for me. Maybe because we'd connected straight away. But it seemed liked we had known each other for some time or perhaps it was family instinct.

Finding Ruby

Anyway, this day I took her down to meet Boy and Doody and Crow. I stood there while they had a really good conversation. Then we got in the car. We went to drive off and as she got back in she said it had been so lovely, she couldn't believe that she had sat there and spoken with Boy. I remember Doodie asking Nance to drop in the next time she came to Bourke.

I left Bourke in 1987 and moved to Inverell, and had lost contact with Nance. It wasn't until 1997 when I was going to Uni at Western Sydney that I caught up with Nance again. This happened through meeting my cousin Jackie Bedford who worked at the Uni. That was when Jackie introduced me to her sister, Carol Kendall. This meeting was very special and will always remain with me as we all became very close during this period and this continues today.

Carol and Jackie had taken me to meet Nance whilst I was in Sydney. We talked about family and Bourke and how we were all related. It was like we had known each other for a life time. It was also interesting to note the resemblance of family members, Nance looking so much like Aunty Ruby both in her appearance and in her mannerisms. Carol and I looking alike. Jackie so much like her cousin Maureen except for the red hair.

During my teacher training at Western Sydney, I invited Carol and Nance to attend one of my lectures where I was to do a group presentation on welfare. Both Carol and Nance were guest speakers and spoke about their experience with welfare and the treatment of Aboriginal children and families. It was real emotional as well as educational for all of us, including the lecturer and other members of the group.

Since this time Nance and I have stayed very close. We keep in contact with each other by phone, and she comes to see me when I'm in Sydney for a meeting or for the Aboriginal State Conferences.

It's been a real journey for Nance as well as for me as I have come to know her and to learn about the experiences she has had in trying to find her mother and family.

Aunty Ruby is my Mum, Nita Knight's, sister. I remember Aunty Ruby working at the Hospital in Bourke as a domestic. She always worked hard and always provided well for her children. Aunty Ruby used to be a cranky old bugger sometimes! Yet she had a good sense of humour. She used to torment and tease you about boyfriends and stuff like that, or someone you didn't like, or whatever. She was a real good person and well respected in the community by both Aboriginal and non-Aboriginal people.

Aunty Ruby had a big family, so did my Mum. There's 15 in my family. Aunty Ruby and Mum came from a family of 14. And we're a very close family, always have been. We all grew up together and spent a lot of time at each other's homes. We are all still very close and always look forward to seeing each other when we meet.

One life, two stories

Reading Nancy's story, and looking at some of those papers – it makes you really think about what happened back then. You wished you'd been there for her. I wish I had been. Because she's so special, and she has been so strong and committed in her search for her Mum and family.

When Nance was searching for her Mum she told me about speaking to my Mum and other family members – my Aunty Alice, and Aunty Eileen down in Dubbo. She spoke with them about Aunty Ruby her Mum. She said that she knew there were family members who knew about her and she wanted to find out more so she followed what lead she had until she finally met with Aunty Ruby.

After speaking with my family and other family members, I think Aunty Ruby really did know who Nance was but found it difficult to tell anyone her story. I think it would have been hard for Aunty Ruby in a lot of ways. How to explain to your other children that you hadn't known your daughter for so long, that you hadn't seen her?

There are members of Nancy's family that have accepted her and there are members that are still finding it hard to come to terms with.

Crow (Paul), he's a character! He rang us one Christmas Day and I said, 'Have you spoken to your sister Nance lately?' He said, 'No, I haven't got her phone number.' So I gave him the number and anyway he rings her, and says, 'I've gotta ring my old sister up and see how she's going.' Then Nance rings me back, she was so excited. She said, 'Lynette, guess what? Guess who just got off the phone to me!' She said, 'He only had a few dollars and you could hear them dropping down the phone.' She loves Crow.

It would have been really good if the family could have come together – I think it's hard for them. I'm sure Crow would have loved to come down to see her, but you know, with finance and the distance too, he's not able to do that.

There is a lot of history that is not spoken about regarding family and kin. Aunty Gladys, who is now deceased, knew a lot about the Edwards family. Mum doesn't say too much, only bits now and then. We had a family reunion in Cunnamulla a couple of years ago before my Aunty Gladys died. She talked all about the family tree and where the family lived and grew up and worked. She also talked about our tribal group which is Kunya.

I told Nance when I went down for her exhibition at Parliament House that Aunty Ruby was Kunya. That's our tribal group on our mother's side of the family. She was proud to hear that because she didn't know what her tribal group was. They're from Queensland, not NSW. The Edwards family, they're originally Queenslanders from the Cunnamulla area. From what I can gather, our grandparents worked on a property called Tinnaburra on the other side of a little town called Enngonia. It's between Enngonia and Cunnamulla and it's the most beautiful property. When we went to that

Finding Ruby

reunion, we went up there to have a look at it. You wouldn't believe how beautiful and peaceful it was. You felt part of it.

I'd say Aunty Ruby would have lived there as a child. One of my Aunties was telling me that they travelled around, working on different stations in that area. They would go down as far as Deniliquin and to Quilpie, places like that. They would have worked on a lot of properties and stations.

It's my understanding that most of Aunty Ruby's children grew up in and around Bourke and as they got older and married, they moved on. I was about eight or nine I think when most of the family moved to Newcastle. Aunty Ruby went down too and she lived down there for a long time but they moved back to Bourke in the 1980s, around 1984. Aunty Ruby died in Bourke – I think she always wanted to go home, to her own place.

Listening and reading Nance's story was very emotional and hard to understand why this happened and why it took so long to find information and answers. She has been so strong throughout all this and continues to show her love towards her mother whom she had only known for such a short while.

I wish we could have met sooner and been closer to each other and for Nance to be given the chance to get to know her family. I wish I'd known earlier. I think if I'd known earlier, even though Nance is much older than me, we could have made things easier for Nance.

Nance's own children now need the support to get to know the extended family. I think it's important for them because otherwise it's another lost generation. They're not going to know their family.

When I look back at what the old Welfare Board and the Government of the day have done to Aboriginal people, I can see how detrimental this has been on many families. What they did to kids back in those days was just appalling. Reading some of the documents from the archives and seeing what they wrote up about the kids, what they wrote about Nance – my goodness! I was thinking if they'd known her mother, how clean she was, how she looked after her kids, how she worked! None of that's mentioned. It's just all judgmental stuff. It saddens me to see that and you just wish the world was different.

I love Nance dearly, you know, and some of the things that have happened in her life I can relate to things that have happened in my family's life. Like when the kids were sent to the institutions for petty things, how their lives changed when they returned. Sometimes they'd be gone for years to an institution just for wagging school. And when they came back they were just so different. It would take them a while to just settle into family. I can see that with Nance, too. Like, she doesn't want to push herself onto family because she wants to be accepted in a way that she can fit in. She doesn't want to just to come in and say, I'm here. She wants to be able to get to know the family and to understand what happened and be accepted.

One life, two stories

Knowing Carol and Jackie, working with Link Up and having that knowledge about Link Up, and having other family members that have been adopted out, I can understand. Like my brother who's just found his daughter after 27 years. He'd been searching for over 10 years, 10 to 15 years, for her. He finally found her and that was through Link Up. Link Up's been the best thing ever for Aboriginal people, to be able to find family. It's also word of mouth, the Koori grapevine, they call it. When you're talking with family, you seem to learn more and more all the time.

Nancy and I were sitting talking about members of the family and I hadn't realised that there'd been a sister that died. Her name was Christine, Aunty Ruby's daughter. My sister knows quite a bit about the family being the eldest. I was telling Nancy about our grandparents, Lena Fisher and Percy Edwards. My sister was telling me that she's got a copy of the death certificate, and it said that Lena was buried under Fisher. I said, 'But why?' She said, 'That's what I want to know, because she was actually married to him.' So there were things that were never written up properly.

The other thing is too, when you hear the name Edwards, obviously you prick your ears and you say, are you related? Where do you come from? Who's your family? Who's your mob? I think that's the only way you find out.

Nancy's has been on a very long journey finding that out. All of her life she's been on that journey trying to find out where she came from, who her family members and her mother were. She's come a long way. Nancy is a very strong woman. Very strong. She loves her grandkids and her children and she worries about not wanting to hurt others including her family. But she wants them to understand what's happened.

I really believe this book is going to highlight Nance's journey, not just for the family but also the community. It's heart wrenching, up front and factual in every sense. There's some happy times, some sad times, but it all needs to be told.

Nance, in my eyes – and for other members of our family – you are the image of your mother.

You will be part of my family always,

Love Lynette

Lynette (Knight) Sheather is Nancy's first cousin, her mother's sister's daughter.

Finding Ruby

Ten lively grandchildren later ...
Back, from left: Mark on Peter's shoulders, then Glen with Gemma, Luke, Tricia Brian in front of him.
Front from left: Kelly, Albert and David in the centre front.
Photo: Mervyn Bishop (2001).

The pain persists

Nancy's life was shaped by her loneliness and the constant search for her mother. She was sure that finding her mother would bring her the sense of belonging and meaning that she had been denied by constant moves. When she found Ruby, it was not the rushing into one another's arms that dreams are made of. The pain of removal is not just something that children have gone through – mothers were also deeply traumatised.

In 1996, as the HREOC Reporting process was underway, Mick Dodson, the then Aboriginal and Torres Strait Islander Social Justice Commissioner, reflected on ABC Background Briefing (11 February 1996):

> The stories ... are very, very painful to listen to, but I think the thing that strikes me most is the absolute cruelty of the practice, you know what I mean? It is devastatingly cruel to do this to a people. It's not just the individual child who was removed or their siblings that were removed, and the cruelty that that does, it's the effect particularly on the mothers. It's the cruel effect on the mothers.

Denial – and the secrecy this entails – is a common way in which people deal with their experience of trauma. Also on Background Briefing, psychiatrist, Jane McKendrick, commented:

> There are feelings of guilt and self blame on both sides, and it's commonly mothers, but I suppose mothers or fathers, who feel that it's their fault, that it's something they did that caused their child to be taken; and even though they know that this was an official policy and that they hadn't done anything wrong, and that their family tell them they hadn't done anything wrong, they still can't get this idea that it was their fault out of their mind. And similarly, the child who's taken away often feels as if it's their fault, that they did something wrong, or they were ugly or something and their parents didn't want them, even though as adults they've been told that this wasn't the case, that it was official policy. And I think this is because it hasn't really been acknowledged by authorities that these policies were deliberate.

In this final sentence McKendrick put her finger on the issue that had become controversial at the federal government level – the need for an official apology.

It is the *acknowledgement* that it was deliberate, racist and cruel – a policy which Stuart Rintoul (2007) referred to as the most evil in twentieth century Australia – that enables Aboriginal people to move beyond self-blame and start the healing process.

Nancy spoke of how her own life was transformed by the official apology from the New South Wales Parliament: "The best thing that ever happened to me was being able to stand up in Parliament to receive that apology." She spoke of feeling privileged and honoured to have been asked to accept the apology on behalf of the thousands of people in New South Wales alone who had been through the traumas of removal.

Being a mother

Nancy loved her three children dearly but she also carried with her the knowledge that some of the problems they came to face as adults resulted from what she saw as her own inability to mother them well when they were young. She was always there for her children but she had to struggle to support them at the same time. As she gave more and more energy to speaking publicly about her own experiences, she would talk about how difficult her own childhood had made it for her to be the mother she would have liked to have been. She had been denied a positive and stable experience of being mothered, and without the modelling and support of a loving family she was on her own when it came to caring for her children. Human beings don't 'naturally' know how to parent. We learn from being parented and from the support of families, for better or worse. The consequences of not being parented well are far reaching. Nancy spoke of how hard it had been for her two sons and her daughter, not having an extended family life and rarely having economic stability. This was reflected in the difficulties she could see them facing in parenting their own children. The trauma and loss became intergenerational.

In 1988, the first of Nancy's 10 grandchildren was born. He was the first of many welcome additions to Nancy's family.

I was there when my first grandchild, Megan's son, was born in 1988. We decided to call him Peter Goodgebah, Peter after my son and Goodgebah means strong man or strong warrior in his other grandmother's language. He was such a very important little person for this Aboriginal family. It was just so wonderful. My Peter ran to the labour ward, nearly knocked 'em over getting there. He'd picked the baby up without even checking if he could – we all laughed but I was a bit miffed – he'd got the first nurse of my first grandchild!

Becoming a grandmother was just wonderful. My little family was growing.

I was on night duty when Luke was born so I couldn't get over to the hospital to see him. There were about 8 or 9 of us who'd been on night duty at Cumberland Hospital and we were having a cup of tea in the nurses' home when, next minute, someone brings out a bottle of champagne. I'm not a drinker – half a glass I'm gone – so by nine o'clock I was pie-eyed on this glass of champagne, running around with this Aboriginal flag tied around my head. My fellow nurses decided they were going to name him: 'We're all working in the field of health. What about we call him Luke the physician?' When I saw Megan the next day, I told her and she liked it too. Luke Burri. Burri means night, he was born in the night. Brian was so fair when he was born we called him Goonama which means 'snow' in Gandangarra.

And there's David's kids. Glen was number two grandchild, He was a premmie, born at Brewarrina and they flew him to Sydney. His poor young mother was left up there without him. I was there at the Children's Hospital in Randwick, waiting for him and this bundle in cotton wool and silver paper just whizzed past. I couldn't even see him, that's how tiny he was. His poor little mother hadn't nursed or even seen him when she came down a few days later from Bourke. Finally we got him home to Brewarrina and I had to hand stitch all his clothes because you couldn't buy clothes that small.

David was born in Bourke and he wasn't well, a 'failure to thrive baby' they called him, a tiny, skinny little thing. His Mum was getting blamed for not being a good mother so I went up to Bourke and found she was really sick herself. Her temperature! She was burning. I told the hospital staff: 'You have the hide to say she's an incompetent mother! She's not a well mother.' And they had her put in hospital then, which meant David picked up too. Albert was born in Brewarrina when I was working in Sydney and I didn't get to see him until he was a fat little thing. Then we got our bright and imaginative Kelly. And when Mark was little, I thought he was the most beautiful child I'd ever seen. Adorable – and mischievous! Then Gemma, our sportswoman and dancer, and my youngest one, Tricia, who'd charm the socks off anybody.

I feel quite fearful about their future at times. I'm frightened that it will end up that way again, that they'll take them and they'll separate them from each other. I'm frightened for my little girls' and boys' futures. That's why I took my grandson to the protest march. I think they've got to be educated in that side of survival. I think they have to learn there's alternative ways to keep going, that you can do something about it. I mean 'people power.'

I think about all the things that they could do, sports, teaching, law, different things come to mind when I look at them, but then I don't really mind what they do, I just hope when they grow up they are able to be happy.

But it's hard. In my anxiety to prevent the removal of my own grandchildren, I'm putting myself into an early grave. It will take a few more generations until this is worked through. For now, I've just got to let people know, know about the hurt but also let them know that we have survived.

But it can never make up for the loss.

Some people have commented, of those children who were taken away, that they had opportunities they would not have had if they were brought up by their Aboriginal mothers on the stations or 'missions' of the Aborigines Welfare Board. As Nancy asserted, this was not her experience. Her own siblings, brought up by her mother under repressive Aboriginal policy regimes, nevertheless achieved a great deal in their chosen fields, including nursing, opportunities that Nancy herself had been denied. It took Nancy a lot longer, on her difficult and lonely path, to find and follow her dreams.

The latter years of Nancy's life were a new struggle. Not only did she want to help her grandchildren through their lives, she was committed to telling people her story, helping them to understand, pleading with them to ensure that 'it would never happen again', that Aboriginal children would no longer be taken from their Aboriginal world, away from their families, even their siblings, to be fostered, institutionalised or adopted into a world in which they did not belong and one which really didn't want them. Amidst constant anxiety, and the worry of finances, failing health and immobility, these are the years in which Nancy nevertheless became well-known through her efforts to bring to other people the stories of the trauma of removal and to ensure it must never happen again.

Nancy took every available opportunity to share her experiences at universities, schools, public functions and rallies. She became a strong and

The pain persists

Nancy, friends and family with her celebratory Citizen of the Century plaque ready to go to Canberra, 2001. Photographer unknown.

well-known advocate for 'the Stolen Generations', for Aboriginal children still having problems with schooling, with the law, and for Aboriginal parents who needed so much more support if they were to overturn the sadness of their family lives.

In 2001, on the centenary of the Commonwealth of Australia, the Federal Parliament called for nominations for 'Citizens of the Century'. Once accepted, the person nominating them would prepare a montage about that person and these, as huge cardboard cut-outs in human form, were spread across the lawns of Parliament House so people could walk among them and learn of their fellow Australians.

Nancy and the Queen at the opening of her exhibition in NSW Parliament House, Sydney, 2001. Nancy and the Queen had something in common as the only female non-members of Parliament to have spoken on the floor of the House. Photo by Gaynor Macdonald.

It was Lynne Ridge from my nursing days who nominated me as a Citizen of the Century, but she didn't tell me about it. She was pretty excited when she found out it had been accepted – so was I. I was very proud, very touched and it was a wonderful experience to participate in it. It was such fun to participate. We hired a bus and took all the kids down to Canberra to see it. Mark told the kids at school the next day that he'd been to another country for the weekend. They had such a good time.

In 2002, an exhibition on Nancy's life was curated by Fiona Nicoll and Ricardo Peach for the Liverpool Regional Museum (Nicoll and Peach 2002). It was also shown at New South Wales Parliament House later the same year.

In her catalogue, Fiona reflected on the exhibition's significance to everyone involved:

Fiona: Nancy's aim is for people to reflect more deeply about what we mean when we advocate 'the best interests of the child'. 'The best interests of the child' is the principle that has guided past and present welfare law reform in Australia. The history of the Stolen Generations require us to consider some challenging questions such as 'Who does the child belong to?' and 'Can it ever be in the interests of the child to be removed from his/her place of belonging?' It is the responsibility of every Australian to contemplate these difficult questions so that another generation of stolen children never comes into being. There must never be another generation of non-Aboriginal people able to turn a blind eye to mental, physical, sexual and cultural abuse perpetrated by those charged with protecting 'the best interests of the child'.

... Nance is deeply offended by having to continually justify her version of her own history while the reputations of the non-Aboriginal individuals who committed these crimes remain untarnished. However, in spite of their anonymous authorship, these documents testify powerfully to the abuse and neglect she experienced as a child trapped within a system that was justified on the basis that it would protect her from this fate. Nance describes her feelings when she saw her documents for the first time:

Nancy: [I felt] nervous, apprehensive, almost to the point of feeling sick. And when I started to go through [the documents] I realised they had a totally different slant on what happened to me. They had reported it in such a way that I could hardly believe what they were writing about me. What angered me the most about the documents is that they almost ignored the rape and child sexual abuse. They were blaming the victim [and] making out that [my] problems were too big and that it was all my fault. I find it unbelievable that they couldn't understand why my behaviour was the way it was. I was angry. I was grieving. I was lost and desperately wanted to find my family. I find their comments on typical Aboriginal behaviour [and features such as] "thick-lipped and sullen skinned" – all these derogatory marks – insulting. Absolutely insulting!

Fiona: As you make your way through the exhibition, you may struggle to reconcile Nance's story with the views of those who were in control as a child and a young women. At various time she was labelled by welfare authorities as 'uncontrollable', 'delinquent', 'sensitive about her race', 'half-caste', 'quarter-caste', 'octoroon', 'serial recidivist' and 'member of a despised race'. However you will also notice the range of views that officials and foster parents bought to Nance's 'case'. Some are compassionate and perceptive while others are obviously racist, cruel and judgemental. Rather than try to reconcile all those different stories, the exhibition aims to bring an awareness of the conflicts between cultures, values and political agendas, which produced the tragic experience of the Stolen Generations (Interview with Fiona Nicoll, 2002).

Looking back on the exhibition, Nancy reflected:

I think one of the reasons it meant a lot to me was because of the way it brought so many of the special people in my life together. So many people played a part in it and even the grandchildren were able to participate in setting it up. I found it very frightening at first. I was telling stories I'd never told anyone before. It was scary because I knew people would come and see it, not just ones I regarded as friends, but others who mightn't think so well of me.

And when they opened the exhibition – it was Andrew Refshauge [NSW Minister for Aboriginal Affairs] who opened it – one very special moment for me was when Val read her poem, My Dad. It's very moving when we share our experiences of being removed with each other.

> My Dad
> Who was he?
> This sad old man
> With tears rolling down his cheeks
> Arms reaching out, calling my name
> As he was chased away.
> Years later I saw this sad old man
> Lying in a hospital bed
> With no more tears rolling down his cheeks
> No more calling my name
> As I watched this sad old man
> Tears rolling down my cheeks
> My heart filled with sadness
> And love for him.
> This sad old man was my dear old Dad.

What was Dad's crime to have suffered so much?
What was my crime to have suffered to much?
What was my crime to have been taken away?
The only crime, that I can see
Was the colour of our skin.
Val Wenberg

I was really quite surprised when the Liverpool City Council asked whether I'd accept their award. I can't tell you how proud I felt about this particular award. Not only for me, but for the Aboriginal community in general. It was a wonderful day, it was just an amazing day. I'm glad the kids were there, it's something we can always remember. We were part of this very important award.

I'm proud of the other achievements, and pleased that I have been recognised in the Liverpool area, because that is the place I've made my home.

These various achievements simultaneously celebrated Nancy's efforts in testifying to her trauma and provided her with a forum for making political statements. Ultimately, however, they have not achieved Nancy's goal of changing the system which had allowed these things to happen. After Nancy's death, her grandchildren were separated from each other in various ways and have had to try and reunite.

In the last years of her life, Nancy's prime focus was her grandchildren. All she wanted, all she strove for, all she worried about each day was what would happen to her grandchildren when she died. She and Peter had become the carers for David's seven children, and after Pete's death (in 2003), it became even more of a worry. She used to say it was the worry that was keeping her alive, when what she really wanted was to be able to give up her struggle.

One of her greatest challenges was keeping the children at school as they got older. She wanted her grandchildren to receive a good education, to enjoy learning, to do well and to succeed at school. She wanted them to have the educational opportunities she had been excluded from as a child.

Social Justice Commissioner, Mick Dodson (1995:26), has acknowledged how difficult things are for so many Aboriginal families throughout Australia:

> It is facile and dishonest to pretend that many of our kids don't get into trouble. ... Given the circumstances they are born into, the

stack of disadvantages against them, they are not doing too badly. Any group of young people growing up in our world, with our socio-economic profile, would act up and get into strife. Lay the veneer of history, prejudice and cultural disjuncture over their starting point and the problem deepens.

During Nancy's speaking engagements she began to speak out passionately about the removal (suspension and exclusion) of Aboriginal children from school. She believed schools were using suspensions to rid themselves of their responsibility for Aboriginal children who were not coping well with the cultural and social demands placed on them in the school environment.

Despite Nancy's input into the schools her grandchildren attended, this seemingly modest aim proved difficult to achieve. As we worked on various projects with Nancy – this book, photographs for the museum project, her guest talks and lectures – she was invariably accompanied by one, sometimes two, of the boys who had been suspended from school. As they got older the suspensions became more frequent. Indeed this is the case for many Aboriginal children. Aboriginal boys in high school are three times more likely to be suspended than other students, 629 short suspensions per 1000 compared to 188 for every 1000 non-Aboriginal boys (AECG 2006:3). Although the Department of Education has reduced expulsions, it has acknowledged that this has been at the cost of an increase in suspensions. Children who have been suspended, often for over two weeks, return to school further behind their classmates, and struggle to catch up. This produces further frustration and anxiety for the children, and exacerbates tensions with their teachers.

A report commissioned by the Aboriginal Educational Consultative Group in 2006 maintained that "It is obvious that suspension will have a significant and detrimental effect on any student's performance" (AECG 2006:4). What this report does not state (but could have) is that 'playing up' is often a response, as Dodson pointed out, to the demeaning position these children already feel themselves to be in. Rather than being a punishment, suspension can become a desirable release from an environment that has become oppressive and punitive rather than interesting, tolerant and supportive.

Nancy had an astute understanding of the difficulties Aboriginal people encounter because of the non-acceptance of their cultural differences. She argued that many of the reasons for suspension, such as swearing, are trivial. The AECG report agreed: 'In many ATSI families and communities, high levels of swearing are regarded as normal and teachers should view it within this context' (2006:9). This may be a fraught issue for schools – but it is not one which will be solved by suspending students.

There is nothing 'inevitable' about the pattern of suspensions and poor performance on the part of so many Aboriginal children. It is possible to break this cycle. In 2004, the Queanbeyan South Public School reported that suspensions involving Aboriginal students had dropped from 80 percent of all suspensions to around five percent, despite the number of Aboriginal students increasing (www.daretolead.edu.au). This phenomenal achievement demonstrates what can be done by a school that explicitly targets 'self-esteem, cultural pride and knowledge, socialization, parent involvement, early intervention and better parenting'. Queanbeyan South's Principal, Paul Britton, sought to counter the ideology of negative difference that permeates Department of Education materials. In describing them as facing economic and social disadvantage, teachers are already perceiving Aboriginal children as 'different', which is all too easily turned into 'less competent'. He explained:

> We have always believed that to make things better for our Aboriginal students we need to work on our non-Aboriginal students because they are the ones giving them a hard time. Getting rid of the racism that develops when you focus on differences rather than similarities has had a big impact on the number of negative incidents at our school.

Nancy could see from her own experience that suspensions were directly related to poor educational outcomes and the loss of opportunity. As she knew, a high percentage of children (42% in 2011) in the juvenile justice system are Indigenous, and Indigenous Australians are grossly over-represented in the adult prison system. She frequently expressed concerns to us about the frequency with which the police patrolled her street and followed the older boys, as if waiting for a chance to pounce.

Chris Cuneen, Professor of Justice and Social Inclusion, cited in Ting 2011, understands the over-policing and incarceration of Aboriginal people, including juveniles, as a mode of 'governing through crime.'

> In this society of increased surveillance and heightened fear, "the problem of crime" becomes a central focus ... Punishment, which is increasingly targeted at those at the margins, becomes the most politically expedient response: it allows politicians to look like they're doing something without the need to consider the longer-term repercussions.

So what do you do with so-called problem populations if you're ideologically not prepared to take a social democratic, social welfare response?

The solutions have to start with educating Indigenous students so they have the same choices that other Australian children have.

... the rise of control through crime has had a profoundly racial dimension in Australia, and the indigenous population has borne the brunt of this ... Racialised punishment is not unique to Australia but its ferocity surpasses some of the most notorious international examples.

Racialised punishment at a juvenile and adult level follows racialised suspensions which impede good education and in many cases follows racialised 'removals' of children from their families. There are decades of neglect and discrimination to overcome. As Nancy often pointed out, it will take more than a generation or two to undo the damage.

As time went on Nancy became angrier and more distressed. As well as phoning and writing to anyone she thought may be able to help, her lectures and talks became pleas to stop the victimisation of Aboriginal children. Nancy did all she could to keep her grandchildren at school and spent time at the schools the children attended advocating on their behalf. She was articulate and feisty and although she had good relations with the school, the community, and some police, the good relationships she had built up with the schools were jeopardised by her anger and frustration.

By 2005 it was clear that Nancy's health was failing. Knowing that publication takes time, the University of Western Sydney produced a short print run of Nancy's book. A wonderful day of celebration was organised by the University on International Women's Day 2005 to launch the book and celebrate Nancy's life. Nancy delivered a powerful impassioned speech for which she received a standing ovation. Former Prime Minister, Gough Whitlam, and the Vice-Chancellor of the University of Western Sydney, Professor Janice Reid both spoke. Professor Reid reflected that:

Admission to the University of Western Sydney enabled Nancy to follow her heart and study nursing. Her excellent academic record and subsequent accomplishments make the negative assessments of her ability as a child all the more shameful. Years of being told she was not good enough left her doubting herself. At University she was able to develop the intellectual, social and professional skills to begin to put this behind her. Nancy's story, told with great courage, reminds us that we should not accept the limits others place on our potential.

Members of Nancy's family were there, including one member of her reunited family, which thrilled her. The majority of people who came,

The pain persists

Former Prime Minister of Australia, Gough Whitlam, wheels Nancy out of the University of Western Sydney – to her delight. Mr Whitlam had made a stirring speech in response to Nancy's story in the commemorative book. Photo: David Marshall, University of Western Sydney (2005).

Aboriginal and non-Aboriginal, were those whose lives Nancy had touched, perhaps some, like our own, irrevocably changed by the need to bear witness. What we, as her co-authors shared with her in the later years, and now write about on her behalf, was her passionate and untiring concern for the ongoing welfare of Aboriginal children.

Nancy passed away on 9 May 2006.

After Nancy died, the seven grandchildren she had been caring for were soon separated. The Department of Community Services took over and Nancy's worst fears were realised. Two of Nancy's grandsons, too old to be put in care, moved back to live with their Aunt. One child ran away, afraid he too would be taken. Three of the younger children were placed with a foster family. This would have broken Nancy's heart all over again. A year later their Aunt had not been told where they were so she was unable to visit them.

But Nancy's influence, and her message, continue to compel a response, even many years after people first heard her speak.

Her ability to reach out and touch people stemmed from her amazing intellect, her excellent grasp of issues, and her ability to bring her own experiences to life in the imagination of her listeners, transforming her personal experiences into a social issue. This was evidenced in Bruce Gaudry's retirement speech as Member for Newcastle and Parliamentary Secretary, made nearly 10 years after he had heard Nancy address the NSW Parliament (NSW Legislative Assembly, Hansard, 22 November 2006:4633):

> I have had the privilege through my role as Parliamentary Secretary to the Deputy Premier and the Ministers for Police, Emergency Services, Education and Training, Aboriginal Affairs and Planning to travel throughout New South Wales to listen to community needs and represent the Ministers and Government and its programs. I particularly treasure my contact with the Aboriginal community, which has yet to share fully in the benefits of this State. Its resilience in difficult circumstances and its work towards reconciliation uplifts me. I will never forget the day that Mrs Nancy de Vries addressed this House on her experience as a member of the stolen generation.

Parliament House tribute 11 May 2006

> Any of us who were in this Chamber on the day when Nancy spoke will remember the emotion with which she addressed the gathering, but, more important, the sentiment and emotion felt by all honourable members. This Parliament has proudly led the way on reconciliation by offering the first apology to the stolen generations.

The pain persists

It is appropriate today that we reflect on Nancy de Vries, who was such a great ambassador for reconciliation and who wanted black and white Australia to find its way forward and grow through a profound understanding of the need for reconciliation. We thank Nancy and her family for what she contributed. Our thoughts and prayers are with them (Mr Brad Hazzard (Wakehurst).

Mr Speaker: In view of the historic significance of the contribution of Nancy de Vries to reconciliation and her address to this Chamber, I ask the members and officers to stand as a mark of respect. *Members and officers of the House stood in their places.*

(Tribute to "Aunty" Nancy De Vries www.parliament.nsw.gov.au/ prod/ parlment/hansart.nsf/V3Key/ LA20060511008).

Each time Nancy told her story, the pain resurfaced and had to be dealt with all over again. But it was her willingness to speak of her own trauma and to take the risks this involved for her personally that was one of her most outstanding strengths. It was the most important contribution she could make for herself, other traumatised Aboriginal people, and for us all, as members of a nation that must come to terms with its own history. Understanding is not enough without the willingness to bear witness, to move beyond intellectual understanding, to feel the pain that will stir us to action.

I received a letter from Siena Perry I want to include here. I would like other Aboriginal people, the Stolen Generation in particular, to read it. Siena's a student of Gaynor's at the University of Sydney and she'd heard one of my talks. I was very touched when I saw this letter. It expresses well the sort of response that I was hoping to receive through telling my story – understanding.

Dear Auntie Nance

Rossiter said 'there is no pride without shame'. As citizens of a nation we have incurred obligations with our citizenship. As a citizen of Australia I am ashamed by what the government did to you and so many others, and I believe it is my obligation to feel sorry. I feel such shame and sadness for you, especially when I see a government that is unable to properly acknowledge the wrongs of the past. I am ashamed that so many people who held power over you in your life abused this power and I am so worried that the abuse will live on as it resonates through families in Australia. I am sad you only got to meet Ruby once.

I am sorry that the authorities intended to breed out your people, culture, history, heritage and blood. And I am doubly sorry that they did this while operating under the guise of 'protection.' I am ashamed that, like you said, some people knew why you were always crying and yet never did anything about it,

I am sorry that we do not learn stories like yours at school. And at university we treat them as examples of the 'subaltern' and the 'voice of the minority'. That we are so scared to confront the human horror of the Stolen Generation, and so confused by our ambivalent and violent emotions towards your story that we turn it into intellectual discourse.

I am sorry that continually the justice system of Australia fails Aboriginal people and minority groups. Like the young man 14 days overdue to be released from prison, who finally killed himself, the son of a Stolen Generation survivor. I am ashamed that this abuse echoes through generations and now that it is perpetuated but through more subversive and subtle controls. I wish these things had never happened to you, or to anyone.

I wish to eradicate my fear of the other, so implicit in my inherent racism, which I regret I cannot deny.

Ronald Wilson said, 'It is not too late to gain release from the burden of this shameful history' and I sincerely hope that you find release from your burden. As you said, I cannot ever understand the loneliness of your childhood. But I hope that you realise that you could never be alone now – you have touched so many people.

Yours truly,

Siena Perry

The pain persists

Anna, Gaynor, Nancy, Jane at UWS launch, 2005. Photo: David Marshall, University of Western Sydney.

References

Aboriginal Legal Service of Western Australia (ALSWA) 1995. *Telling our story: a report by the Aboriginal Legal Service of Western Australia on the removal of Aboriginal children from their families in Western Australia*. Perth: Aboriginal Legal Service of Western Australia.

Abrahams, Melissa 1998. Bringing them home or taking them nowhere: the Federal Government's response to the National Inquiry into the Stolen Generations, *The Indigenous Law Bulletin* 4(9), February: 15–16.

AECG Issues Paper, June 2006. Suspension and Aboriginal students in NSW "One Size Does Not Fit All". Stanmore, NSW: NSW Aboriginal Education Consultative Group.

ANTAR 2001. Australians for Native Title and Reconciliation (ANTAR). www.antar.org.au.

Beckett, Jeremy 1988. The past in the present, the present in the past: constructing a national Aboriginality. In *Past and present: the construction of Aboriginality* (ed. Jeremy Beckett). Canberra: Aboriginal Studies Press.

Council for Aboriginal Reconciliation (CAR) 1997. *Renewal of the nation*, Highlights of the Australian Reconciliation Convention, 26–28 May (video).

Dodson, Michael 1995. *Aboriginal and Torres Strait Islander Social Justice Commissioner Third Report*. Canberra: AGPS.

Edwards, Coral and Peter Read 1989. *The lost children*. Sydney: Doubleday.

Felman, Shoshana and Dori M Laub 1992. *Testimony: crisis of witnessing in literature, psychoanalysis and history*. New York: Routledge.

Felman, Shoshana 1992. Education and crisis, or the vicissitudes of teaching. In Felman, Shoshana and Laub, Dori MD, *Testimony: crisis of witnessing in literature, psychoanalysis and history*. New York: Routledge.

Felman, Shoshana 1993. *What does a woman want? Reading and sexual difference*. Baltimore: John Hopkins University Press.

Four Corners 1996. *Telling his story*, Documentary on Rob Riley. Broadcasted on 15 June 1996.

Hall, Catherine 1996. Histories, empires and the post-colonial question. In *The post-colonial question* (eds. I. Chambers and L. Curti). New York: Routledge.

Hall, Richard 1998. *Black armband days: truth from the dark side of Australia's past*. Milson's Point, NSW: Vintage Books.

Healey, Justin 2001. The Stolen Generations and the need for a national apology. In ed. J. Healey, *Issues in society: towards reconciliation*, Vol. 140, Rozelle, NSW: Spinney Press.

Herron, John 2000. Extracts of his submission to the Senate Committee on the Stolen Generations, *Sydney Morning Herald*, 4 April.

Huggins, Jackie 1993. Always was always will be. *Australian Historical Studies* 100, April: 459–64.

Huggins, Jackie 2001. *Working the walk*. Armidale: University of New England Press.

Human Rights and Equal Opportunities Commission (HREOC) 1997. *Bringing them home: report of the National Inquiry into the Separation of Aboriginal and Torres Strait Islander Children from Their Families*. Sydney: Commonwealth of Australia.

Individual Heritage Group 1987. *La Perouse: the place, the people and the sea*. Canberra: Aboriginal Studies Press and the Cultural Politics of Otherness, Social Analysis 27:50–69.

Langton, Marcia 1993. *Well, I heard it on the radio and I saw it on the television*. Sydney: Australian Film Commission.

Lattas, Andrew 1990. Aborigines and contemporary Australian nationalism: primordiality and the cultural politics of otherness, *Social Analysis* 27:50–69.

Laub, Dori MD 1992. Bearing witness, or the vicissitudes of listening and an event without a witness: truth, testimony and survival. In Felman,

References

Shoshana Felman and Dori Laud MD, *Testimony: crisis of witnessing in literature, psychoanalysis and history*. New York: Routledge.

MacIntyre, Stuart and Anna Cook 2003. *The history wars*. Melbourne: Melbourne University Press.

McClements, J 1961. *Report of The Honourable Mr Justice McClements, Royal Commissioner appointed to inquire into certain matters affecting Callan Park Mental Hospital*. Sydney: Victor CN Blight, Government Printer.

McRae, H, Nettheim, G, Beacroft, L, McNamara, L 2003. *Indigenous legal issues commentary and materials* (3rd edn). Sydney: Lawbook Co.

Moriarty, John 2000. *Saltwater fella*. Ringwood, Vic: Viking.

Morrison, Toni 1988. *Beloved*. London: Picador.

Mudrooroo, Narogin 1990. *Writing from the fringe: a study of modern Aboriginal literature*. Melbourne: Hyland House.

Nettheim, Anna 1996. A crisis of response. BA Hons Thesis, School of Sociology, Culture and Communication, University of New South Wales, Sydney.

Neville, AO 1940. *Australia's coloured minority*. Sydney: Currawong Publishing.

NSW Department of Aboriginal Affairs (DAA) (n.d.). Background briefing: introducing Indigenous Australia. Available at: www.daa.nsw.gov.au/publications/Fact%20Sheets.pdf, accessed 22 Feburary 2012.

NSW Department of Education and Training 2005–2010. Long suspension and expulsion summaries. Available at: www.det.nsw.edu.au/about-us/statistics-and-research/key-statistics-and-reports, accessed 22 Feburary 2012.

NSW Education and Communities (EC) 2010. Long suspension 2010. Available at: www.det.nsw.edu.au/media/downloads/about-us/statistics-and-research/key-statistics-and-reports/long-suspension-expulsions-2010.pdf, accessed 22 Feburary 2012.

Open Day Committee (ODC) 1990. A brief history of the Rozelle Hospital, Sydney.

Read, Peter 1995. Don't turn your back on me: a bibliographical review of the literature of the Stolen Generations, *Aboriginal Law Bulletin* 3(73), April.

Read, Peter 1999. *A rape of the soul so profound*. Sydney: Allen and Unwin.

Reynolds, Henry 1989. *Dispossession*. Sydney: Allen and Unwin.

Rintoul, Stuart 2007. Apology 'must say removals were evil'. *The Australian* December 17. Available at: www.theaustralian.com.au/in-depth/aboriginal-australia/apology-must-say-removals-were-evil/story-e6frgd9f-1111115129855, accessed 25 May 2012.

Rudd, Kevin 2008. Speech by Prime Minister Kevin Rudd to the Commonwealth Parliament. Available at: www.dfat.gov.au/indigenous/apology-to-stolen-generations/rudd_speech.html.

Taylor, Charles 1991. *The ethics of authenticity*. Cambridge, Mass.: Harvard University Press.

Ting, Inga 2011. Aboriginal crime and punishment: incarceration rates rise under neoliberalism. Thursday, 15 December. Available at: www.crikey.com.au/2011/12/15/aboriginal-prison-rate-continues-to-rise-is-neoliberalism-at-play/, accessed 21 February 2012.

Trinh, T. Minh-ha 1989. *Women, native, other: writing postcoloniality and feminism*. Bloomington: Indiana University Press.

Wharton, J Cheyne (ed) 1911. *The jubilee history of Parramatta: in commemoration of the first half-century of municipal government, 1861–1911*. Parramatta: TD Little and RS Richardson.

Wilson TJ 1997. *In the best interest of the child? Stolen children: Aboriginal pain, white shame*. Link Up (NSW) Canberra: Aboriginal History.

Wolfe, Patrick 1994. Nation and miscegenation: discursive continuity in the post-Mabo era. *Social Analysis* 36:93–152.

Young, Iris Marion 1990. The scaling of bodies and the politics of identity. In Young, Iris Marion. *Justice and the politics of difference*. Princeton, NJ: Princeton University Press.

www.ingramcontent.com/pod-product-compliance
Lightning Source LLC
Chambersburg PA
CBHW071115160426
43196CB00013B/2580